Heart to Heart

With

Robert Wagner

Ex-Library: Friends of
Lake County Public Library

Heart to Heart

With

Robert Wagner

Diana Maychick and L. Avon Borgo

ST. MARTIN'S PRESS
NEW YORK

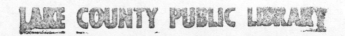
LAKE COUNTY PUBLIC LIBRARY

17490616

HEART TO HEART WITH ROBERT WAGNER. Copyright © 1986 by
Diana Maychick and L. Avon Borgo. All rights reserved. Printed in
the United States of America. No part of this book may be used or
reproduced in any manner whatsoever without written permission
except in the case of brief quotations embodied in critical articles or
reviews. For information, address St. Martin's Press, 175 Fifth
Avenue, New York, N.Y. 10010.

Design by Amy R. Bernstein

Library of Congress Cataloging-in-Publication Data

Maychick, Diana.
  Heart to heart with Robert Wagner.

  1. Wagner, Robert, 1930–   . 2. Moving-picture
actors and actresses—United States—Biography.
3. Television personalities—United States—Biography.
I. Borgo, L. Avon. II. Title.
PN2287.W235M38 1986   791.43′028′0924 [B]   86-3939
ISBN 0-312-36413-X

First Edition

10 9 8 7 6 5 4 3 2 1

For our families

Contents

Acknowledgments

Although this book is by no means an authorized account, Robert Wagner did speak with us before the project began. On those occasions, his charm and kindness, his unfailing dedication to his craft, convinced us he was due a biography. What came across in our meetings, what we hope shines through the book, is the beauty of his efforts to survive.

For patiently submitting to our questions, we'd also like to thank his friends, family, and colleagues, most especially Lionel Stander, Gerald Browne, and Harry Thomason.

For laying the groundwork for our sleuthing, we are indebted to Hedda Hopper and Louella Parsons and all the other Wagner chroniclers who preceded us and upon whose pieces we relied.

Heartfelt gratitude also goes to Mike Hall, Welton Smith, Georgette Deveney, Mark Goldstaub, Jim Mones, Blanka Nedela, Jerry Tallmer, John Carmen, Stephen M. Silverman, Tom Dunne, Margaret Schwartzer, Laurel Gross, Ann Ambruster, Jami Bernard, Ruth Hunter, Dan Aquilante, Bernice Doyle Sampson, Shannah Goldner, Ruth E. V. Salley, and the entire staff of the *New York Post* library, especially the ever-helpful Jack Begg and Chris Bowen, and the staff of the Billy Rose Collection at the Lincoln Center Library for the Performing Arts. We must also thank Spiros Stanpolapulos, a Greek shipbuilder who spoke with us outside Athens about R.J.'s love of the sea.

One special note. Writing a book turns you into an awful friend, a worse family member. Ours know that. The party, so to speak, was always over by the time we got there. Christmas dinners had to be reheated. We slept through other special occasions. So we would like to offer our apologies and our love to Stella Maychick, Margot and Vico Borgo, and Damon Borgo. And to Joe Leiper, Thomas King Flagg, and Jim Stark (our three favorite bachelors); Debra Fine-Yohai, Carlo de Pretis, Carmen Fabella, Adele Donham, Jay Butterman, Charles Skinner, Barbara Pflughaupt, Roz Kupcakli, Janet Santos, Phil Fishler, Marianne Carcenac, Ed Broderick and the rest of the folks at WPG, all we can say is we're back in the world. Until the next one!

It's easier to work with someone who knows what he's doing.

—Samantha Smith, (1972–1985),
on working with Robert Wagner.

Heart to Heart

With

Robert Wagner

1
Smooth Operator

A brunette in tight white stretch pants and bad, red stiletto heels gingerly eases under the thick hemp rope that separates her from Robert Wagner. Prime time's prime steed is in Washington, D.C., to film episodes for the "Lime Street" TV series and the ladies are going wild. "I just have to meet him," the brunette begs the balding Washington policeman whose primary duty this day is to keep the fans at bay. "I would do *anything* to meet him," she says. Her eyelashes flutter in supplication. Her bottom wiggles. She heaves her noticeable chest. That last gesture does it.

The policeman corners Wagner while he's knotting his tie for the first scene of the day. "Do me a favor R.J.? I know you're busy, but my friend, she, well, she would do anything to meet you." They look at each other man-to-man: the six-foot-tall, crisply handsome, fifty-five-year-old Wagner and the paunchy policeman. He's in his fifties, too, but he's lived a life where the years show. Wagner breaks into a grin that reveals teeth so even and white they look like dentures (they're not). "Bring your friend over," he says. "Anything to oblige."

Like a lot of American women, she wants to hold Wagner's hand, not shake it, so she palms him limply, and then just doesn't let go.

"I've loved you since 'It Takes a Thief,' " she begins.

"Not before?" he asks, then laughs.

She doesn't get the joke. "Well, I didn't know you before that." She looks flustered. "I'm sorry about Natalie, I mean . . ."

"Where do you live?" Wagner asks, immediately changing the subject. "Oh, Virginia is a pretty spot. Kind of slow-moving and polite. I like it there. Do you have a garden? Things grow so well in Virginia. If you have the time. Do you ride? Well I do. It's a lot of fun."

A production assistant gives the signal to clear the set. "You know, you're even nicer in person. It's been a pleasure talking to you, Mr. Wagner," she says, heaving her chest again.

"Call me R.J.," he says, extracting his hand. "And the pleasure's been all mine, all mine."

It's no wonder women swoon for Wagner. He's as polite as Alexander Mundy from "It Takes a Thief," as wry as Pete Ryan from "Switch," as worldly as Jonathan Hart of "Hart to Hart," and as good a single parent as he is on "Lime Street." "When it comes down to it, I'm playing myself up there," he says. "Different aspects of me. A conventional character on the outside who's unconventional underneath." Says his good friend Gerald Browne, the best-selling novelist: "In real life, he's more like Cary Grant than Cary Grant himself."

Unlike Grant, Wagner's TV shows have made him more accessible to the "regular folks," as he calls them. "Lime Street" co-producer Harry Thomason attributes Wagner's popularity to "this incredible sex appeal. It's not rough-and-ready allure. It's the champagne kind."

It's domestic bubbly, though, mass-market effervescence. Like Ralph Lauren's Polo pony insignia, prime time's prime steed offers the possibility of sharing surface elegance with "the regular folks," the loyal Bud drinkers, the A & P shoppers.

Wagner does not shop at the A & P (although his loyal housekeeper, Willie Mae Worthen, sometimes does). He is not a beer drinker, preferring Italian and French wines, and Northern European varieties, too, until he "read in the *Times* the Austrians processsed their grapes with gasoline." With the more than $2 million a year he pulls in from his TV performances, the bulk of it coming from syndication rights to his old shows, Wagner is not down-home. But those who are assume he came from their ranks, and not from a privileged background as the only son of a steel industry executive.

"For whatever reasons, people think they can imitate me," he says. "It's this 'if he can do it, I can do it' thing. It's great for me, that kind of identification. I think a lot of people would like to be doing what I'm doing up there and I give them a little vicarious pleasure."

Offscreen, his life-style surpasses those of his TV characters. His own good times at his five-bedroom ranch-style home in West Los Angeles are filled with the mighty and the mightier. Paul Newman and Joanne Woodward, friends since 1969 when they all made *Winning* together, are often dinner guests. "Jill [St. John, his constant companion] usually does the cooking," he says. "We're the guinea pigs for her TV segments on 'Good Morning America.' " Cary and Barbara Grant drop by frequently. When he's back East, Wagner and St. John visit her old flame, Henry Kissinger, and his wife, Nancy, at their Connecticut retreat. This isn't name dropping, this is Wagner's life. Sir Laurence Olivier has been a good friend since the days he cast Wagner and Natalie in his production of "Cat on a Hot Tin Roof." Other legends surface: his mentor Spencer Tracy; Clark Gable, the guy who got him his first screen test. "A lot of my old friends, well, they're gone," he says quietly.

He doesn't mention Natalie, but there are constant reminders of her death. While shooting the scene on the Potomac, the "Lime Street" cast and crew are forced to abandon a seaplane and swim the polluted waters to safety. Wagner observes the mishap from a nearby speedboat. His stunt double, Greg Barnett, is stepping onto the plane's pontoon when the captain gives orders to abandon the plane. "It happened like that," R.J. says later. He snaps his fingers. The plane, a lightweight $70,000 Cessna, sank in a matter of minutes. "Thank God they could all swim," he concludes. Everybody else is thinking of The Accident four years ago on Thanksgiving weekend. All R.J. does is lower his eyes; his haunted look tells the story.

Back in his hotel suite, he turns into a celluloid version of the movie mogul. He tells "Lime Street" co-producer Thomason that "everyone was well protected during the accident. No sweat. God was with us today." He accepts a script from his associate Carole Feitler, who, he says, "reads and reads and reads for me. Soup cans, cereal boxes, anything that might make a good movie." He pads across the room in clogs to show his guests a present from Frank Sinatra. "Sinatra convinced me to come the last time I was here [in Washington]. For the inauguration show. We put it on twice: first for the President. Then for Mr. Bush. It was great, really pumped up. But the weather, remember? There was a blizzard. The weather was going sideways." He returns from the bedroom in a sea of tissue paper. "Sinatra gave one of these to everyone who participated." The paper drops. Delicately, he displays a white baseball warm-up jacket embroidered in gold thread with a picture of the White House. "It's real silk," R.J. says. He gets a call from California. He makes a call to a florist to send a bouquet to a young actress who didn't get a part. He doesn't stop.

His friends assume all his busy work is to keep his mind off The Accident. "Ever since Natalie died, R.J. has become engrossed with every aspect of the business," says his pal Gerald Browne. "He loved being with her. Every time I flew to the coast, I'd call up R.J. 'Let's have lunch,' I'd say. Wouldn't you know it? I'd drive all the way out to their place in Beverly Hills and he'd always pull the same thing. 'Nat's making a picture out at Univeral' or somewhere. 'She'd love to see you. They break for lunch soon.' So we'd take a long drive and eat in some awful commissary. You see, he just couldn't stay away from her. R.J. was very possessive and she could do things with those big, brown eyes! She was fun, she was flirty. For R.J., Natalie was the grand, grand passion. I don't think there was anybody else for him." "He'll survive," says Lionel

Stander, his West Los Angeles neighbor and "Hart to Hart" co-star. "But R.J. will never get over what happened."

If work really functioned as an antidote to mourning, Wagner would have been over his loss in a week. Besides "Lime Street," in which he stars as well as co-produces, he has a deal with Columbia Pictures TV that includes "movies, long-term television, several series, half-hour comedies, everything. Total," he says.

There's more. He's talked to another old friend, Elizabeth Taylor, about doing a remake of the 1932 tearjerker *One Way Passage.* And writer Joan Tewkesbury has asked him to produce her version of Calvin Tompkins's *Living Well Is the Best Revenge,* about Sara and Gerald Murphy, the American expatriots who lived in France as if every day was an event, the couple who became the basis for F. Scott Fitzgerald's *Tender Is the Night.* "Fitzgerald was their friend," R.J. says about the writer's scathing portrait of the Murphys as Dick and Nicole Diver. "But he was a writer first, I guess." It's been rumored that Wagner and Natalie themselves became the grist for a writer friend's mill fifteen years ago when their former secretary, *The Boys in the Band* scenarist Mart Crowley, wrote *Remote Asylum,* which was about shallow film stars and their tedious circle.

One of the three phones in Wagner's hotel suite rings again. An Elton John minion is on the line. Wagner wants some of John's music for one of his projects. Into the mouthpiece of the phone, he launches into a rendition of the stripper's theme song: *Da da DA, dadada Da. Da da dah . . .* Wearing only a pristine white terry-velour robe provided by the hotel and serendipitously embossed with a big R (for the hotel, the Regent, and not for R.J.), Wagner accompanies his own humming with a sort of sitting dance, crossing and uncrossing his legs in time to the rhythm of bump and grind.

Robert Wagner must have the best legs in the world: long, svelte limbs of enticement with rounded calves and slightly dimpled knees. They are better than his old friend Betty Grable's ever were, dotted as they are with fetching beauty marks, especially one coy black circle in the niche under his kneecap. His legs are tan, as is the rest of him, which accentuates the feeling that you're staring into two pools of Caribbean Sea when you look into his eyes. He's worked too hard, with too many debilitating failures to his credit, to look this good at age fifty-five, but he does. As his buddy Lionel Stander puts it, "R.J.'s almost too pretty to be a man."

As a contract player in the fifties, a perennial yes-man to all the studio moguls who cast him in forgettable pictures, he starred in a lot of bombs. Audiences didn't care. He became their Brooke Shields. In 1952, he started "getting five thousand letters a week. ▓▓▓, in those days, I just did what I was told. You'd get your call in the morning, go to this lot, that lot. A lot of the time, I didn't know what movie I'd be doing before I got there." Mention the movie he deems his worst, 1954's *Prince Valiant,* and it makes him howl. "That goddamn wig! ▓▓▓, I was bad. With my body stocking and my rubber calves, and the wig, that goddamn wig! All the people from New York acting schools used to sit in the balcony for that one. To throw popcorn!" R.J. is uncharacteristically slurping his coffee. "Oh, I forgot my singing sword! How could I? Can you imagine! All that, for the sake of being seen."

What kept him going then, and still keeps him going, is that "the audiences keep coming back to see me. That's been my biggest compliment: they still want to watch me."

Pouring Pouilly Fuissé for the guests in his suite, offering brie and crackers, lighting cigarettes, R.J. shows some of the suave stuff that his fans have come to expect. But old Hollywood didn't give him the opportunity to perfect his smooth persona, the up-starts in TV did. "In the sixties, everybody was an anti-hero. There weren't many parts for a guy like me. I was under contract with Universal and Lew Wasserman called me into his office one day. From his drawer he pulled out a copy of *TV Guide.* 'This is where you belong,' he said. 'You'd be great in this medium.' I wasn't interested. 'No way,' I said. I guess it was generated by anxiety. I was basically scared. I was getting a little tired of failure.

"But of course success changes your mind a little. I'm ready to take risks, ready to do shows like 'Lime Street,' where the small domestic moments are as important as the chase scenes. The family scenes are what sold me on the show."

Although there was never any possibility of his own children co-starring in the new series—"they'd crucify me for nepotism" —Wagner says he's recommended the business to his three daughters, twenty-two-year-old Kate (from his second marriage to Marion Donen), fifteen-year-old Natasha (the product of Natalie's second marriage to producer Richard Gregson), and twelve-year-old Courtney (his only child with Natalie, from their second marriage to each other).

"You should see Courtney's Madonna," he says. "She puts on Katie's garter belt, gets a flashlight for a mike, and belts it out, twirling, dancing, lots of lace. . . . I think all my kids are going to go into show business. Absolutely. But I want them to develop character first, so that if they act, they can develop characters. Still, it's going to be damn hard, you know, being the daughters of Natalie and myself."

He tries to keep them away from publicity hounds, "down on the farm, so to speak," among his four cats, several dogs, Arabian horses, chickens, quail, and grouse. "It's good for the girls to have responsibilities. I mean, they go to all the concerts, Prince, Boy George, Michael Jackson, all the ambiguous, what do you call it, androgynous singers. But then the girls come home and they're responsible for the animals.

"I've even built a pigeon tower," he says. "I love those birds."

When they were first dating, Wagner gave Natalie a bracelet with a charm engraved "Wow, Charlie." They'd picked up the expression from *On the Waterfront,* in which Marlon Brando tended pigeons to keep the awful world from closing in on him.

In a phone conversation later, we try to tell him the pain of loss eases with time. "Good," he says. But his voice has cracked.

R.J. doesn't break down often anymore, and it comes as a shock that the suavest man on TV hurts inside. Most of the time, he tries to hide his grief behind his signature smooth facade. It works. In his presence, it's easy to feel among Hollywood's chosen. But unlike a lot of his contemporaries, R.J. worked a lifetime to get there.

2

The New Face

The coolly sophisticated R.J. made his first appearance as an actor in drag. He didn't don the sequined sheaths favored by Dustin Hoffman in *Tootsie* or the dark stockings and pumps his friend Tony Curtis relied on to cover hairy legs in *Some Like It Hot*. Flash wasn't necessary to pull off the woman he was portraying. Besides, her legs didn't show anyway.

R.J.'s initiation into the profession that would exert a stranglehold on him for the next forty years was as a woman noted for her somber skirts and white bonnets. In a high-school production of Longfellow's "The Courtship of Miles Standish," he played Priscilla Alden, the popular Pilgrim who admonishes a would-be suitor (later her husband) to "Speak for yourself, John." It was an embarrassing debut for this tall, athletic kid. There were snickers in the school auditorium, no doubt, but there were also cheers. R.J. would receive that kind of double-edged reaction to his performances for the rest of his long career.

Someone once asked him what he would do if he were out of movies. Without missing a beat, he said, "Try to get back in." On the surface, it makes sense. Here's a guy who's currently secure in his work, recognized by millions of fans. The remark begins to resonate with deeper import, however, when the totality of R.J.'s forty years in the business are examined. On the whole, there's been more pain than pleasure. In some of his lowest downswings, he's often had to fight hard to "try to get back in." Yet R.J. has endured to become one of Hollywood's most familiar faces and now boasts one of the world's biggest fan clubs as proof.

He was not born into the industry. Robert John Wagner, Jr., arrived on February 10, 1930, in Detroit, Michigan, a city devoted to another big American industry, automobiles. It may not have had the glamour of Hollywood, but it equaled it in money. Neither element much impressed little R.J. All he wanted to do was go to the movies with his parents and come home and mimick what he'd seen on the screen. Said his sister Mary, "I knew then that he was going to be an actor."

Wagner, Sr., a well-to-do steel company executive, transplanted his family to Beverly Hills when R.J. was nine. The place where dreams come true was at its height of wish-granting in the early 1940s, when the Wagners settled into the city of fantasy and found themselves surrounded by the world's greatest thespians. R.J.'s movie-going habits increased, and he fed his imagination in other ways as well.

His introspective side, still very much part of his personality today, had its roots in his California childhood. "I was a very aesthetic kid," R.J. recalled. "I liked paintings and antiques. I used to help refinish furniture and help with the display in an antique shop. I read a lot, too. I still read constantly. I was crazy about Robert Louis Stevenson, stories about the sea, about horses, Zane Grey. I ended up spending most of my time in the movies. I used to try to jump over the wall of the Fox Studios and watch 'em make pictures. Basically, I was a romantic kid. I still am."

Weekends and holidays in Palm Springs were especially pleasing. Near what is now congested Bob Hope Drive in the sunny resort, the young R.J. would dart in and out of the date groves hunting rabbits and rattlesnakes. "We used to come down here all the time, Mom and Dad and myself," he said. "We all had horses. We'd trailer them down and spend Christmas. It was wild country then. Unbelievably beautiful. Rudolph Valentino had a place. So did Sam Goldwyn, Harold Lloyd, the Zanucks, Edmund Goulding. This is where they all came to get away from the power plays of Hollywood."

During high school, he needed to retreat as well. The teen years are notorious for turning minor problems of adjustment into high drama. His own puberty was no different. Despite the fact he wound up popular enough to be elected president of his 1948 Santa Monica High School graduating class, he had a tough time. R.J. experienced real-life drama as he was shunted from one military school to the next. "That's what was callously done with rich kids in those days," he once said. But the fact remains, he didn't blame his parents for succumbing to the standards of their class. And for the most part, his growing-up years were nearly idyllic. In 1968, he described them with fond remembrance: "I grew up in California at a time when the San Fernando Valley was nothing but two or three big ranches. I had horses. You could ride, it was all open. I practically lived outside."

It was one of the few uncomplicated times in his life. R.J.'s personality has always been a cross between the active enthusiast and the passive yet intensely interested observer. These separate and distinct features of his character have been both a hindrance and a boon to his career. On the one hand, his relentless pursuit of his goal to become an acclaimed actor has always served him well, saving him when his talents were being disparaged. His urge to analyze and re-analyze a role, his passionate studiousness, have also helped him perform his parts convincingly and efficiently. On the other hand, this kind of zeal would lead him to be typecast for many years as the lowest form of Hollywood's necessities, the pretty boy. Finally, his need to break a role into its distinct elements often led him to overact when it came time to put all those parts back together again for a performance. He has always lacked a certain spontaneity necessary to make a role come to life. R.J. has spent an entire career trying to rectify these problems, and to a large extent he has achieved his goal.

Over the years, when talking about his acting, R.J. would be given to speaking in a variety of poses. During a 1968 interview, he took on the manner of an Oriental philosopher: "I used to be conscious of the arrival, therefore I lost the journey," he said. "Lately, I've been working more on the journey than the arrival." Or: "The trouble was, I had an idea of what I should project, instead of being it." In later years, during his second marriage to Natalie Wood, when his life was more balanced, his thoughts would become more coherent. In contrast, the early R.J. leaves the impression that everything he said was for the purpose of self-promotion. But looking closely at his life during those years of intense struggle and self-doubt, it's easy to understand R.J.'s need to impress the public and his peers. Much to his chagrin, he was not often taken seriously.

R.J.'s career began by accident in the late forties. A Doubting Thomas, he didn't really pursue acting until after he witnessed the lives of movie stars. At about age fifteen, R.J. wangled himself a job as a caddy at the exclusive Bel-Air Country Club. It was a typical job for a wealthy young man out to make some pocket money, but it would change R.J.'s life. At the club, he met the likes of Clark Gable, Alan Ladd, Fred Astaire, and Randolph Scott, all relaxing over drinks, sharing insiders' bon mots, and talking in whispers about deals and pictures. He wanted to be part of that club-within-a-club, too. A few years later he recalled, "My father was pretty upset when I took a job as a caddy at the club. But it was there, when I toted golf clubs for Gable, Randy Scott, Fred Astaire, and John Hodiak, that I decided I wanted to be an actor. I thought they were very special people."

R.J. constantly pestered the stars for their advice on how to get into the business. The actors, it seems, liked him a lot. But all he got out of the experience were lots of autographed photographs, which are still proudly displayed in his home. One's inscribed from Clark Gable: "Go, Boy, Go!" it says. And go he did.

"But it really wasn't so easy," he confided. "I went to Warners in 'forty-seven and they were going to use me, but they had a big strike, so I went back to school, then to work with Dad [in the steel business.]" As a second backup, he joined the Marine Corps reserve. Still, he didn't forget his true goal. On weekends, R.J. took a job polishing airplanes at a field where he knew many stars and producers kept their private craft. One plane he polished belonged to brawny character actor Brian Donlevy. He gave R.J. a five-dollar tip for the shine, but it wasn't free money. "Here, good-looking," Donlevy told R.J., "go get yourself a book on acting." Ever earnest, he did buy an actor's manual. But it wasn't R.J.'s style to study the profession. "Learning to act from a book was like learning to ride without a horse," he said.

He remained true to his heart, though, and continued to aspire to a film career, but not without first having to strike a deal with his father. Wagner, Sr., gave R.J. just one year to break into the movie business. That would be the limit of his tolerance. While looking for that first part, R.J. agreed to spend his spare time visiting the various steel mills around the country to see how he might fit in. Wagner, Sr., and Chat, R.J.'s mother, were proud of him, but they were also a bit perplexed at his first career choice. Sure, they had a fine young man for a son. Intelligent and incredibly handsome, six-foot-one, brown eyes, brown hair, and a superb athelete who shone at tennis, water-skiing, squash, even Ping-Pong, R.J. was everything a parent could wish for. How could he want to fritter away his life on a juvenile whim? He had to prove himself.

But hunting for that first role proved fruitless. The year dragged on, and no part turned up. R.J. was desperate. Visions of years behind a desk in an office with a view of a steel mill loomed up in his frantic mind. His bad dreams had him ending up as president of the Bel-Air Country Club. He had to do something.

As it turned out, it was his father who got R.J. his first part after all. Wagner, Sr., was a well-connected man and a pillar of the community. One of his acquaintances was tough-guy director Bill Wellman. As R.J. explains: "After Dad sent me to the various steel mills and found out I just wasn't going to amount to anything in his favorite field, he asked Mr. Wellman to talk to me." After a casual chat, there turned out to be a small part for R.J. in Wellman's next movie. It was *The Happy Years,* an adaptation of Owen Johnson's Lawrenceville Stories, about a turn-of-the-century young prankster's misadventures at prep school.

R.J.'s first and only part since his high-school days as Priscilla Alden did not mark an auspicious beginning. "I had only one line to speak and my face was hidden by a baseball catcher's mask," he recalled, adding what would become his refrain of the next fifteen years: "It didn't do much for me, although I did learn a lot from Bill Wellman's direction." It was the answer he used often about an unrewarding part. He thought it showed he was conscientious and probably easy to direct. It showed he was enthusiastic; but it also showed, frighteningly clearly, that R.J. was often too eager to please.

After *The Happy Years,* however, R.J. was out of work again. During this period he held all sorts of jobs he would never have needed if he had gone into the steel business. There was even a miserable stint as a dishwasher. But the kid was determined to succeed, and the one thing R.J. has proven he has is willpower.

When it first "happened," he didn't need determination. One night, at a Beverly Hills hotel restaurant where he was having dinner with his family, he was "spotted." As the story goes, he stood up to sing some impromptu songs for the other guests. Agent Henry Wilson saw him and decided he had found something. Perhaps. There were also reports that some of Wilson's golfing chums clued him in to Wagner's existence. This would not be too surprising, given the kind of movie titans who would again and again "out-of-the-blue" come into R.J.'s life, take him under their wing, and, in effect, save his career.

The day after Wilson made his "discovery," he took R.J. down to 20th Century-Fox and gave him a screen test. Darryl F. Zanuck saw the test. He was the kind of production executive who once said about himself, "I decided to become a genius." He liked what he saw in R.J. and, on the spot, signed him to a $150-a-week contract. A newspaper heralded the deal with the headline: "Marine Lands Seven-Year Contract."

It seemed to him like the major leagues. Not only did the agreement call for his salary to increase through options to $1,000 per week, R.J. had a judge approve a plan to save 20 percent of his salary. In celebration, he went out and bought himself a Cadillac. A few months later, he came to the realization that he could not afford it. It was a rude awakening. "I was making like a movie star," he recalled, "when I was just a bit player."

The deal placed R.J. on a nearly outdated road—he was on his way to becoming one of the last Hollywood "buildup" stars. The buildup was for untrained but physically attractive young people who the studios believed had a future. Rock Hudson, Tab Hunter, Troy Donahue, and Tony Curtis were among his colleagues. When the moment was ripe, the studio would launch one of these prodigies into a leading role on a wave of publicity. The possibility of such attention was dangled in front of each young man as the ultimate in studio largesse.

R.J.'s first duties, however, were less glamorous. He made screen tests "with every pretty girl some producer or executive thought would be screen material," he said. "It was terrific experience. I listened and observed as the girls were coached, and it was priceless help." R.J. continued his screen testing even after he finished his first movies, *Teresa,* with Pier Angeli, and *The Halls of Montezuma.* Dropping by the offices of the drama coaches at Fox, he always had one request: "Have you got a test you want me to do today?" he'd ask, like a vagabond looking for odd jobs.

In fact, R.J. was always eager to learn whatever he could of the business. He made friends with the electricians and learned about lighting. He also dropped in on the makeup and wardrobe people and made friends with them as well.

As it turned out, there was good reason to put himself through these routines. In his first dramatic scene in 1950's *The Halls of Montezuma,* there was one notable bit that R.J. couldn't get right.

He had been up since 3:00 A.M. studying the script. Hours later, on the set, things were tense. It was close to 100 degrees with the lighting on. While everyone else was sweating and mopping brows, R.J.'s hands were cold and clammy. "Take forty-five," someone yelled with desperation, and R.J. tried once again to get it right. He ended up stumbling through it again. Finally, the exhausted director Lewis Milestone said, "Well, it's no good. But at least it's completed. Print it and let's go home." There was an awful silence on the set. R.J. was devastated. He'd blown his whole career, he thought. Then a reverberating voice sliced through the deadly quiet. It belonged to a beefy technician. "Give the kid another chance," he told Milestone. "Quit pressing, kid. Relax." By all accounts, R.J. calmed down and performed his scene with great skill. The crew burst into applause.

Although it would be years and plenty of analysis before the lesson of the technician would be completely internalized, R.J. would continue to make lasting friends with people behind the scenes. They'd help keep his career rolling in those difficult early years. In part, he attributes his success to them. He later recalled that of the 125 other acting hopefuls then at Fox, he was the only one who made it.

Soon enough, R.J. was jumping from one picture to the next, beginning with *The Halls of Montezuma,* a dark, bloody account of the Marines' heroic exploits during World War II. The movie starred another studio buildup veteran, Richard Widmark, and only Widmark got noticed by the reviewers; R.J.'s performance was largely ignored. But the movie was a box-office success. His next movie, *The Frogmen* (1951), another wartime adventure recounting the operations of the U.S. Navy, was much the same story. That same year, he got a small part in in *Let's Make It Legal,* with Claudette Colbert and MacDonald Carey. He also had a romantic lead in a little-known picture called *Fourteen Hours.*

A pattern began to emerge with the type of roles he got in these domestic romances. They were characters of little depth who hid behind winning smiles. But he had some firm support for meatier parts. His backers, including the once doubting director Lewis Milestone and producer Robert Bassler, were predicting a brilliant future for him.

It seemed they were correct and everything was going along as scheduled when, in 1952, R.J. got rave reviews for a one-minute part he played toward the end of *With a Song in My Heart.* The weepy true story of singer Jane Froman's comeback after being crippled in a plane crash, the movie was demolished by the critics. R.J. didn't care. They all took notice of a fine performance by a young actor. Said one: "[But there were] several appealing moments near the end when a nerve-shattered soldier to whom the singer had once addressed 'Embraceable You' in a stateside nightclub reappears in a German hospital. . . . One Robert Wagner plays the scene with quiet force."

Just a simple line really, but fan magazines took notice. They began to mention the handsome young star, and run a few pictures. They even linked him to Susan Hayward, the leading lady of *With a Song in My Heart.* He said it was bull, but the fans began to wonder just who he was. The letters started to come in, first in a trickle, then, within a year, a flood.

3

Prince Charming

Louella Parsons would show up at Romanoff's for a 12:30 lunch interview while her arch rival, Hedda Hopper, arrived just after Louella left at 1:45. Unbeknownst to either of them, they would be seated at the same table. It was, of course, the best in the house, and each of them felt she deserved it. Waiters rushed to unfold clean linens and lay out new silver. Maitre d's swore staffers to secrecy. R.J. witnessed the whole thing. As a young star on the rise, he felt like he never left that table.

If for no other reason, R.J.'s early days are extremely interesting because they reveal much about a bygone era of Hollywood. It was still the day of the big studios, with stars under contract. Today, actors are largely independent and studios are very budget-conscious. But in the 1950s, there was money to burn. And in a town like Hollywood, where you're forgotten if you linger too long in the bathroom, money was spent on those duennas of gossip, Hedda and Louella. Actors toyed with them at their own risk, as Frances Farmer found out. Still they served an all-important function: they helped prevent the public from "forgetting." Stars flocked to them for this reason. And studios heeded their opinions, busy-bodies and tasteless though they might be, as the barometers of the rise and fall of an actor. It was a power trip, pure and simple.

In the late 1940s, as studios were beginning to pay less attention to building up the reputations of contract players (soon to be an extinct species anyway), managers, agents, and publicists arrived to take up the slack. And often the stars made a lot of use of the

telephone in their own right, calling Hedda and Louella themselves. In the early 1950s, while Joe McCarthy was sending shivers
clear across the country from Washington, newspaper and magazine gossip became a very important area of image creation for
actors, including R.J. Movie stars needed to exude a certain all-
American quality. And if anyone looked all-American, R.J. certainly did. Publications never failed to take advantage of this.

Toward the mid-1950s, things began to cool off again. War
babies were coming of age and the publishing world tried to win
their hearts with a softer touch. "Teenzines" like *Sixteen* and
Tiger Beat flourished.

R.J. spent a lot of time doing what he could to please those who
controlled the gossip. It was the beginning of a long period where
he would go out of his way to please those he worked for. Over
the years, this subjugation of his independence would lead him to
become very inhibited and self-conscious, and often to lose all
confidence. It probably caused his first divorce. It would not be
until the successful "It Takes a Thief" series in the late sixties that
he'd be able to re-emerge fully as himself.

But in the early days, he was definitely a product of canned
Hollywood. He became a smooth talker, but someone who cul-
tivated a charming bashfulness at the same time. "He should be
in the diplomatic corps," said one columnist.

But he really was just a regular twenty-three-year-old. He liked
to go bowling, play records, build miniature trains. He and Debbie
Reynolds were going steady for a while and they often acted out
scenes from movies. Other dates included Susan Zanuck, Debra
Paget (his co-star in *Prince Valiant* and *White Feather),* and
Barbara Stanwyck. "I had a hunch to get into acting, so I did,"
he said with a grin; but his main purpose in life was fun.

Unfortunately, the fun had to be rationed while he spent most
of his free time courting a couple of old-bag gossip columnists. A
good example of the kind of torture the gossipers could put him
through can be found in this passage from an interview that he did
with Louella Parsons in August of 1953:

I asked Bob if he'd like to come and see me after I heard he'd been selected by 20th Century-Fox for the role of *Prince Valiant,* hero of the King Feature Syndicate cartoon which is extremely popular in millions of homes.

I kept Bob waiting over an hour because I was recording a radio show. I expected to find him pouting. Such a spoiled young man wouldn't like to be kept waiting that long, I thought.

Instead of a sour face, he said: "I'm awfully sorry about all the trouble you had today."

Besides the tone of Louella's condescension, which was enough to drive any self-respecting person to distraction, keep in mind the little-known fact that R.J. is fairly tempermental, something he learned to conceal over the years. It must have taken a great deal of restraint on his part not to put Louella in her place. On other days she and Hedda would force teendom's young hero to go shopping with them, to answer any personal questions either might have, and to sit back quietly while they produced inane columns. R.J. bit his lip through all of this and ended up being one of their favorite interviews. In their articles they actually tried to help him. A little charm and a lot of indulgence went a long way with the gossip mongers. R.J. had both in ample supply, and he would use it on Hedda and Louella for the rest of their careers. Even when their power began to wane, he continued to treat them like royalty. If he had no time for anything else, he'd make time for them. His devotion was so complete he even won the heart of Louella's longtime servant, Collins, who "is just crazy about Bob," as Louella was fond of saying.

R.J.'s kowtowing to gossip columnists didn't pay off in movie roles. His parts became slightly more substantial, but they were still not what an actor looks for to boost his career. In 1952, he had memorable feature roles in John Ford's *What Price Glory,* a remake of the World War I adventure, and in *Titanic,* the story of the final hours aboard the doomed ship. He also had a part in *Stars and Stripes Forever,* the story of John Philip Sousa.

In 1953, as the likable but heedless young Greek fisherman
Tony Petrakis in *Beneath the 12-Mile Reef,* R.J. got his first star
billing. He almost drowned in the process. On location in Tarpon
Springs, Florida, during a scene where twenty-five swimmers are
struggling for possession of a gold cross, he was inadvertently
kicked in the stomach by another cast member. R.J. began swal-
lowing water and sinking. Again, the background staff came to
his rescue and a sound-crew member saved his life. The movie
itself was less dramatic. It was a run-of-the-mill account of the
Florida rivalry between Greek immigrant sponge fisherman and
their American counterparts. The critics were not as impressed by
the acting as they were by the spectacular underwater photography.

Even before the picture was released, R.J. had already won the
hearts of thousands of teenagers around the country and was
beginning to show signs of Hollywood-star worldliness, mostly in
his attitude toward the opposite sex. He had mighty definite pref-
erences. "I don't like girls who use lines," he said. "I like girls who
look natural, not too much makeup. I can't stand girls who are
amateur psychologists and start telling me all about myself," he
said. He also couldn't stand girls phoning him. As he put it,
"Aggressive gals leave me cold." Once he found a properly reticent type, he'd avoid Romanoff's and other trendy spots. Instead,
he'd take his date to small, off-the-beaten-path places and listen
quietly to jazz.

He became such a music lover during his early twenties that
R.J. often rehearsed his lines, read, and studied accompanied by
Peggy Lee or Frank Sinatra. These two singers provided the background music in his one-bedroom Beverly Hills apartment as he
began studying heraldic literature in 1953.

Several months later, he took his medieval knowledge and
barged into director Henry Hathaway's office. "Please, sir, I'm
Robert Wagner. I've come to ask you to let me test for *Prince
Valiant.*" Undaunted by the director's grim stare, he continued,
with an excess of enthusiasm, "It's been my favorite strip ever

since I was a kid. I've studied Arthurian legends. I've taken fencing lessons—"

"I see no reason to test you," Hathaway replied.

"Oh," R.J. said, and turned to leave.

"I see no reason to test you for the part," Hathaway continued, "because the part is already yours."

R.J. put all he had into the role. It was important that he do well, that the film as a whole do well. The executives impressed upon R.J. that they could not take any chances with the movie. The comic strip had several hundred thousand ardent fans who would not react kindly if their favorite characters came off less than perfectly. It was equivalent to Christopher Reeve tackling Superman in the 1970s and '80s. Unfortunately, *Prince Valiant* received only mixed reviews. Some critics complained that R.J.'s voice was a dull monotone throughout the entire picture. Others enjoyed the athleticism, dash, and lavishness of the technically innovative CinemaScope-Technicolor production. The box office, for its part, found the movie palatable, and R.J. seemed to be on top of the world. Reporters were calling him the most popular actor in Hollywood. If the fan magazines had anything to say about it, he *was* the most popular actor in the world. R.J. recalled that day when the technician saved the day for him. "I owe it all to him," he proclaimed. When, a few years later, R.J. sought more profound roles and the fights with Fox began, he would come to view *Prince Valiant* as a thorn in his side and even his worst movie.

For now, he basked in the warmth of stardom and took his role of teen idol seriously. R.J. took special care to respond personally to as much fan mail as time allowed. He recalled something Alan Ladd told him back on the golf course: "Mr. Ladd said to remember the people who remember you. If you get fan mail, answer it." He took the advice to heart, and was then leading Ladd in the polls. He still had to dine and coo with Hedda and Louella, but he was no longer solely dependent on their graces.

In the studio commissary, getting a seat near Prince Valiant was a coup for any star-struck young girl. The girls actually fought over the tables. One director said with the sigh of a put-upon father, "At last my daughter thinks I'm wonderful. I got her a table next to Bob Wagner's."

4

Papa Spence

Soon after R.J. experienced his first taste of success, Spencer Tracy became a father figure to him. They first met in 1954 when they worked together in the western *Broken Lance,* the story of Matt Devereaux, a strong-willed cattle baron and his four bickering sons. With Tracy in the lead as Devereaux, R.J. played his most devoted son, Joe, the half-breed. It was a relationship that was also acted out in real life.

Tracy took a liking to the young actor. Even before they met, however, Tracy had had his eye on R.J. He'd seen him in *Beneath the 12-Mile Reef* and had been impressed by R.J.'s enthusiasm on the screen. When *Broken Lance* came up, Tracy specifically requested R.J. For this, the veteran actor won R.J.'s undying devotion. Each day on the set R.J. would watch Tracy's every move as if missing anything, anything at all, would be a sacrilege with dire consequences. Tracy, a crafty codger who could see out of the corner of his eye, noticed that R.J. needed direction. Often, he would stop what he was doing to coach him. R.J. would try very hard to please his mentor. "I was desperate to be an actor," he recalled. "I could mimic all the greats—Cary Grant and James Cagney—and I kept doing things the way I thought they'd do it. Spencer kept saying, 'Don't act; just be yourself,' but I couldn't do it."

R.J. tried to be an "actor," to saunter and put on an attitude. Tracy would have none of this; it only made R.J. wooden, stultifying his natural charm. Even worse, it showed that R.J. was not stretching his capacities. Though he worked hard, he wasn't trying hard enough. "You've got to grow," Tracy kept saying. "You mustn't stand still." R.J. wasn't sure what he meant.

However, the lessons had some effect on the quality of the performance R.J. turned in for *Broken Lance.* Many of the critics wrote that it was his best performance yet and that it was, indeed, fine acting. R.J. himself was proud of his effort. In later years he would describe *Broken Lance* as the only one of the many films he did for Fox of which he was truly proud.

After the filming was done, R.J. took some time off to participate in a pro-amateur celebrity golf tournament. For him, sports have always been a way to let off steam, and he needed to do just that after the wonderful but terrifying eye-opening sessions with Tracy. Golf was a great release. In 1954, he sported a 14 handicap. Shooting a 77, he boosted his two professional partners, Al Besselink and Jay Herbert, into a tie for top honors. Newspapers and magazines everywhere picked up on his exploits.

Trying to cash in on R.J.'s success in *Broken Lance,* the studio next cast him in another western, *White Feather.* R.J. played the lead, a government agent desperately trying to prevent conflict between Indians and gold prospectors. Since there was nothing innovative about the movie and the direction was uninspired, it went nowhere. R.J.'s acting, away from the influence of Tracy, suffered noticeably.

Feeling misgivings about his career, not really knowing if he had it in him to act, R.J. went into his next role with little enthusiasm. *A Kiss Before Dying,* a chiller in which he played a psychopathic killer, was above average fare, but it would have been better as a TV movie. The critics blasted it. R.J. himself termed it "a small bomb," and it left him wondering if things were going to get worse. For a while, anyway, they did. R.J. had a lot of time on his hands. The prospect of having nothing to do is for R.J. similar to a shark that stops moving. When sharks stop moving, they die. R.J. has always been the type who has to keep going, keep working on something, especially his career. The phone was never out of his hand for long.

It was at this time that R.J. recalled what a laconic prop man once told him. " 'The slivers,' the guy said, 'are always rougher coming down than going up.' " R.J. imagined he could feel the tickle that precedes that first puncture as he sat at home certain nights looking at his shelf of Harvard Classics, hoping the phone would ring. What good are the great books, he would think. Paging through Aristotle, Euripides, Shakespeare, R.J. was too impatient to reflect on the wisdom of ages. I'm learning more about life from being an actor than they could ever teach me, he thought. Acting, he said at the time, was an education. You had to do more than just follow the paces and imitate the greats. You had to strain. Otherwise, there was no learning and no getting ahead. The future was appearing to him, and it brought with it responsibility. It was time to be more serious, time to start pushing his talents to a new level.

But he was still a young man whose thoughts centered on fun. He dated nearly every night of the week, but he would not get married, he said. On this point he was adamant. Marriage, he thought, would handicap his career. Besides, as he would say with a devilish grin, "I want to have lots of dates with a lot of girls. I am going to try not to be serious—that is, until I get established."

In his mind, the game was "to get girls." He would try anything, including banging drums and singing. He didn't want to admit he developed these talents only for wooing purposes. Oh, no! "I might have to do some of that in a picture," he said.

He kept in shape and even got himself a Siamese cat named Rudi. It was a nice ploy and he liked him, "but it's just a cat," he explained, "I'm no James Mason" (a feline fanatic). He would cook at his one-bedroom Beverly Hills apartment, using paper plates to avoid having to wash up. However, he had one vice that would make him late for a date: poker. R.J. would stay up all night playing with his friends.

Even while he was fooling around with his buddies, his feelings of responsibility began to weigh in more and more heavily. R.J. would talk about getting himself a two-bedroom apartment. It was a trivial step up, really, but he made more of it. He'd fret, worrying that he wasn't going to be able to afford the new place if things didn't pick up. Even though he really hadn't been out of work for very long, it was a low time in his life. R.J. had been thinking about the things that Tracy had told him. He was beginning to understand how much there is to acting. He was beginning to realize he had been beguiled by the superstars at the golf course into dedicating his life to a difficult, ego-shattering career. But Tracy's concern gave him new resolve.

Years later, R.J. was more revealing about the type of man Tracy was and the role he played in the young actor's life. "He was very helpful. . . . He had deep convictions about people. He believed in me very much and turned me around and made me look at myself. This opened me up quite a bit.

"Genuinely, Spencer Tracy cared about me. At that time I had nothing on my mind but my hair and he made me say to myself 'Hey, wait a minute!' As long as I had my name in the paper and my hair was combed I felt everything was fine. I did as I was told. I was taking no risks, making no contributions. At first I didn't know enough not to be natural," he admitted. "It was when I became aware of acting that I found myself in trouble." During *Broken Lance,* Tracy's good intentions enlightened the young actor as to what was lacking in his own creative impulse. At first, however, R.J. became very confused, and he would remain so for several years.

When the phone finally rang, it sounded like a chorus of angels. "I'm sitting there doing nothing," R.J. recalled, "and Spence wanted me for *The Mountain.* He gave me co-star billing above the title. That got me swinging again." Not only that, but R.J. felt that working with Tracy again was more than just working.

The Mountain was filmed on location in Bavaria in 1956. "I guess that was probably the hardest assignment I ever had," R.J.

said. "We were so far from everywhere, in the Bavarian Alps, and we didn't have all the comforts in the world. I was pretty glad to get back to my apartment after being out of the country so long." To the set of *The Mountain* he brought with him an electric toaster, frying pan, coffeepot, and other assorted kitchen items.

High in the northern reaches of the German Alps, with the elements acting as severe adversaries, R.J.'s domesticity caused muffled laughter from the cast and crew. "Are you here for light housekeeping or to act?" Tracy asked him with a gravelly guffaw. In a way, it was a more than a jibe. Tracy was still playing papa. He wanted R.J. to realize he seemed more concerned about the niceties of his surroundings than the purpose of his being there. He still had a lot to learn.

In the movie, Tracy played a tough, weather-beaten mountaineer who tries to lead a rescue party to the site of an airplane crash on the icy peak of a mountain he has never before been able to scale. He received good notices. R.J., who played his rapacious and cowardly younger brother, fared less well. Critics regarded his performance as "needlessly unpleasant" and "too unrelievedly evil."

R.J. was unfazed. He felt his apprenticeship to Tracy had served him extremely well and that, indeed, his future seemed brighter for it.

5

Serious Business

The phase that R.J. went through with Tracy was undoubtedly an important milestone in his career. Though he did not come out of it happier than he went in, R.J.'s desire to become a star and a respected actor was in earnest, and he continued to put a lot of effort into it. In fact, it was becoming common knowledge that R.J. was a workaholic.

In October 1956, Louella Parsons took note and did a story on R.J. entitled "Robert Wagner—A One-Hobby Man: Work." Cloying and typically patronizing, the piece is a definitive example of the Parsons treatment:

> The only actor I know in Hollywood who hasn't a hobby or some outside interest in a business venture is 26-year-old Robert Wagner. When I asked him the reason, he said, "Acting is my life's work and that gives me no time for anything else."

> This young man, the favorite bachelor of most women from 16 to 60, took me to lunch at Romanoff's and then we went shopping.

> Now I ask you what other handsome young actor would take his whole afternoon off to carry bundles for a woman out of the 16-year-old bracket?

> He helped me select a birthday gift for Walter Lang, who had directed him in 'Song in My Heart' with Susan Hayward.

> That wasn't all the presents we bought that afternoon. Believe it or not, Bob gave me his expert advice on a shower present for Debbie Reynolds.

"Wasn't Debbie once your best girl?" I asked Bob.

"She was indeed," he said. "She's one of the nicest girls I've ever known. But we were just kids when we went together."

If anyone thinks it's easy to be an actor, this should make them realize that there is more to it than smiling for the camera. If done correctly, however, these unpleasant interviews had rewarding payoffs. Louella went on to discuss R.J.'s career and his continuing rise to the top in great detail and, whenever possible, in a laudatory manner. This promotion kept him going, as it would many times in the future. After this and other gushing celebrity profiles in 1957, R.J. got star billing in *The True Story of Jesse James*. This time he also got good critical reviews.

He was now being regularly touted as Hollywood's "most promising young actor," "fastest rising star," and "brightest new face." After working with Tracy, R.J. could not let these remarks go without qualification: "The word star is tossed around too easily in this business. I still have a lot to learn. . . . Now where do I rate with Spence? Certainly not on the same level."

R.J. was also beginning to take life more seriously. He even began to dress sedately: "A fellow can't ask for leading man parts if he wears nothing but blue jeans," he said. R.J. always regarded his profession as a business. On the phone constantly to friends and managers to keep himself as much in view as possible, like all actors he had also gotten himself an answering service. And, mustering his confidence, he moved into that two-bedroom duplex he had been "hankering for" and bought himself every possible new electric gadget to fill it.

He was now undeniably more sophisticated and richer, and perhaps even slightly pretentious. "I don't like to cook regardless of what the fan magazines say," he announced. He required a maid because he had "a habit of tossing things about." He slept in the nude, he told reporters, and had a double bed because "I roll." Also, his temper and moodiness were noticeable to those who knew him. Often he would have a friend over just to have someone there, although sometimes there would be no conversation. "I just like to know there's a pal around," he said. He became somewhat of a self-proclaimed expert on women. "I've never known a girl who doesn't like to eat," he declared. He would denigrate the opposite sex for their vanity. He liked career women, though. "I like a girl to have purpose. I also like girls who are girls."

R.J. was nervous. He didn't know how he should act. In his rush to please, he had forgotten to be himself. He wanted to please someone, but now he did not know whom.

6

Brown-Eyed Rebel

R.J. would now change the course of his life in an irreversible manner. It was not to be his acting or his sports exploits that would now win him teenagers' intense interest, but his first real romance. The young lady in question, only nineteen, was a certified movie star. She'd been in thirty or so movies since she'd first performed in *Happy Land* at the age of four. This star, of course, was Natalie Wood. To understand R.J., there's no better way than to get a grasp on his relationship to this woman with the "mothering brown eyes." Still adamant about not getting married, he would begin to be blinded by an opposite urge.

Natalie insisted she had felt the same attraction years before, as an eight-year-old actress working at the Fox lot. "He brushed right past me," she recalled. "I was just a staring kid as far as he was concerned." Natalie always asserted that right then and there she knew she wanted to marry that "dreamboat of a guy."

In 1956, she was no longer a staring little kid but a dark-haired beauty in Hollywood's best tradition, what was then termed "a fine catch." She had recently completed *Rebel Without a Cause* with James Dean, her first hit after a string of flops including *The Rose Bowl Story. Rebel* got Natalie the attention she needed to be considered for other good parts. The movie startled the public with its portrayal of teenagers as mature people capable of understanding the world's complexities. After it opened, Natalie was dubbed the "teenager's teenager." It seemed to confuse her. "It has been very nice to be called that but I never knew whether it was good or bad," she said. "I never knew exactly what it meant." What it meant was that she was a big star again. It had come in the nick of time.

R.J.'s following was not as large, but it was big enough. And his career had become a lot steadier than Natalie's. This fact belies the notion that, when they started dating, Natalie was far and away the bigger name. However, in the course of their marriage, even though R.J. would make many movies, some of them well received, Natalie's track record would surpass his.

After their first encounter, they accidentally met again at a Hollywood fashion show in 1956. This time Natalie was not "just a staring kid." In fact, many people were staring at her. She wondered if R.J. would remember her, and hoped he'd notice how much she'd grown up. He certainly noticed. On July 20, 1956, he called her for their first date. Natalie would never forget it because it also happened to be her eighteenth birthday. "That evening was very exciting," she enthused. "R.J. turned out to be a terrific date. Aside from his obvious attractions, he has an incredible sense of humor and the evening seemed to fly by, we were having such fun." In fact, R.J. wanted to doubly impress himself on her consciousness. Not only was he sitting next to her in a darkened movie theater, but there he was on screen, larger than life! He'd taken her to see *The Mountain.*

The next day he sent Natalie flowers and called to say thank you. It seemed it would end there. "I'll see you again sometime," he said as he hung up. Natalie was very disappointed. She had thousands of dates but "every time the phone rang, I'd say to myself, 'that must be R.J.'" Five months later, she accidentally ran into him at a CBS awards ceremony. "Natalie, you're too thin," he said. "I have a great diet to build you up. Have lunch with me at the studio tomorrow."

They decided to meet at noon. Natalie turned up three hours late. Incredibly, R.J. was still waiting "and he was not angry," Natalie recalled. "But he's too much of a man to let a girl, any girl, lead him around by the nose. As we started going out more and more, I found him polite, but very unsubtle in his views on my being late for dates and things like that."

By December 6 Natalie had already learned her lesson; she was on time for their second dinner date. It was a night both of them would always remember because, as they revealed years later, it was the evening they made love for the first time.

7

Heart to Heart

Their romance was the sensation of its time, the love affair of the century, the courtship to end all courtships. A year after it began it would end in the marriage of the century, at least in the words of the celebrity columnists. But who had R.J. gotten himself mixed up with? Did she measure up to the type of "girl" he had so painstakingly described as his ideal woman?

Natalie was a capable young lady. She liked to have her say and to have control of her life. R.J. had said he would prefer a career woman over the old-fashioned stay-at-home type. Natalie was also a "girl." She was only nineteen. Moreover, her diminutive stature —five feet two inches—her minuscule weight—ninety-four pounds—and her petite features guaranteed that she would always at least appear girlish. And her ability to affect classic little-girl helplessness was second to none. Twice in her life she had gotten out of contracts by going before a judge and simply saying that she thought her contract was bad. Each time the judge had looked at her and had found that he had no choice but to agree. Natalie's demeanor had that amazing power to beguile that very few women have, even in the realm of the stars.

For her own part, Natalie wanted a man who was strong, who would look like the head of the family, and who had a strong shoulder she could lean on, the kind of man who would want to be her protector. Never mind that she was earning loads of money and was quite capable of running her own show; along with her career she wanted a traditional marriage. And that's what R.J. wanted in a wife.

Natalie had been brought up by a very strict, Old World mother who schooled her in the traditions of family. With the 1960s approaching and new social freedom hot on its heels, she would be hampered by the enormous psychological inconsistencies that two differing world views presented and would need to go through years of psychoanalysis. Finally, she would become liberated herself, after a fashion, but she would never lose the indomitable urge to be a good homemaker and mother. Eventually, she would conquer her problems and realize her desires. But that was a long, long way off.

Inevitably, both of them began thinking about what a life together might mean. In their hearts, both R.J. and Natalie regarded marriage as a tonic, as a way of solving the personal and professional problems that plagued them. For Natalie, getting married had to do with the longing to be independent of her mother, to have a structure that was her own. She was earning all the money, so she felt she should be able to make her own decisions. As long as she hung around with Elvis Presley and led her life in the adolescent fast lane, no one would take her seriously.

For R.J., the reasons were more complex. Marriage, he hoped, would be an anchor for him. It would give him purpose so that he could approach his life and his profession more seriously and maturely. He told himself that marriage would allow him to exude a certain aura that would make him seem more responsible, more capable intellectually and, therefore, professionally. Although he was twenty-seven, his appearance was, as it remains today, much younger than his actual age. Now it's a boon to his career, as it was when it gained him entry into the business, but as he tried to mature professionally in the late 1950s, his boyish looks held him back. Marriage, he hoped, would change him enough to be able to combat this problem successfully. He was also hoping the complexities of marriage would help him overcome what he called the lessons from the "Rin Tin Tin school of acting. You know how they used to handle him?" he asked. "They had this cat in a bag, and every time they took the cat out of the bag the dog's ears would go up. I was a bit like that." In fact, in those early years, people said R.J. could affect only two moods other than smiling: sadness with a frown and surprise with lifted eyebrows.

Moreover, he felt that marriage to Natalie would provide him with a partner in his quest. "We have mutual interests," he said at the time. "We read scripts together and practice. We don't run out of things to talk about."

No one can assert, however, that it was in any way a marriage of convenience or that either one was simply using the other to further personal gains. The love between them was due to the compatability of their personalities and their natural desires for one another; after all, each was very attractive physically. It was true love, young love, and any benefits that were to be gained were simply the by-products of a right thing done at the right time, when both were trying very hard to seize control of their lives. In fact, in separate interviews, each said, "I've straightened myself out," after making mention of meeting the other.

A few months after their courtship began, Natalie went to the Adirondacks resort of Scaroon Manor to shoot the outdoor scenes of *Marjorie Morningstar*. After he concluded he couldn't be without her, R.J. showed up too. He moved right into Natalie's room. Her mother, Marie Gurdin, was horrified. But sensing the changing times, sensing too that she was about to lose her grip on her-daughter-the-star, for whom she lived and breathed, Mrs. Gurdin held her old-fashioned tongue and refrained from comment. She actually put herself through the ultimate humiliation of serving the young couple breakfast in bed. R.J., seemingly less courteous in private than in public, did not protest on behalf of Natalie's mother or attempt to assuage her obvious embarassment.

Not so for the eight-hundred curious guests at Scaroon Manor.

They felt the filming of Marjorie Morningstar's adventures were, as one columnist put it, "much less gripping than the real-life boy-meets-girl drama, 'Will Bob Win Natalie?' "

R.J. haunted the set daily. Clad in jeans, sneakers, and an unbuttoned shirt, his hair matted and long, he looked, said a local reporter, "like a charter member of the beat generation, or an escapee from the Actors Studio." Observers felt he appeared too overprotective of Natalie, but he really just wanted to be near her. They were a terribly young couple, terribly in love. "I want two children, a boy and a girl," she told one newsman, sounding more like a child herself than someone on the verge of marriage. "But right now, I have everything I want," she said, giving R.J. a long, lingering glance. He said nothing.

The youthfulness and the brave self-confidence displayed by these two fledgling adults was heartrending. Keep in mind that even before R.J. had heard of Hedda and Louella and their ilk, Natalie had learned to curtsy to the press. In reality, R.J. was having tremendous difficulties becoming accepted by his peers as something more than a pretty face, and Natalie was already taking sleeping pills because her nerves kept her awake. Alone, each was unable to cope. Together, they thought they would be formidable and happy. They would run their lives as stars ought to be able to run them. It was no accident that each was already a star when they started dating. Anything less and they would not have had the all-important sense of teamwork and understanding. Together they wanted to add up to something more than they had individually, both professionally as well as personally. Without that vaguely subconscious sense of purposefulness, no love would have blossomed.

In the purest sense, they needed each other.

8

Bubbles and Baubles

Transoceanic relationships often force couples to realize that either they want to make a commitment or they don't. While R.J. was away doing studio-required publicity tours, Natalie missed him dreadfully. The feeling was mutual. "He called me all the time," she said. "He had this quaint habit of making his phone calls in threes. He's a great one for oral postscripts. Just a joy to the telephone company! It must have been a rather expensive habit —but I admit I was rather flattered. I think we both realized how deeply in love we were during the time he was in Japan," she said. "Before he left he'd given me a gold charm bracelet and a charm engraved 'Wow, Charlie.' We'd picked up that expression from seeing *On the Waterfront*, and 'Charlie' became our pet nickname for one another. Every day while he was away, I'd look down at the charm on my wrist or at his picture on my night table."

When he returned in the fall of 1957, their relationship grew even stronger. On December 6, the anniversary of their first serious date, R.J. made dinner reservations at Romanoff's, the site of all his public luncheons with the gossip queens. Natalie stopped by his apartment first. He offered a champagne toast to their year together. In the bottom of her glass, Natalie found a beautiful diamond-and-pearl ring. "Read the inscription, Charlie," he said. Inscribed on the band were two simple words: "Marry me."

Later that evening at dinner, R.J. toasted with more champagne. Again, at the bottom of her glass was a precious bauble, this time a pair of pearl earrings. "I was so happy," Natalie said.

"I was laughing and crying at the same time." After the meal, R.J. ordered a third bottle of champagne. Yet again, he had a surprise for Natalie. This time, she found a charm for the bracelet he had given her a year ago. The inscription read: "Today we are one year old."

Before the celebration began, R.J. had thoughtfully made an appointment with Natalie's father, a prop maker, and formally asked for her hand.

Into this time of jubilation crept one jarring note. When Joan Collins heard about their impending wedding, she remarked to a friend, "All the luck in the world, huh? Well, he'll need it with that dame!" Everyone who overheard looked at her as if she was crazy or jealous or both. This was going to be one of happiest occasions in Hollywood.

So as not to interfere with Christmas, the young couple chose Saturday, December 28, 1957, as the date of their wedding. At 5:00 A.M. the night before, Natalie, R.J., and a small group of friends arrived in the quiet resort town of Scottsdale, Arizona, where R.J.'s family had moved. The couple picked Scottsdale "to get away from the Hollywood-type wedding," R.J. said. Just before midnight, their friend actor Nick Adams knocked on Natalie's door to deliver R.J.'s wedding gift. The heart-shaped diamond brought tears to her eyes, and the note bowled her over. "I miss you. What are you doing tomorrow around one o'clock?"

Adams then took Natalie's gift to R.J.. It was a stick pin with a heart-shaped diamond. "Darling," Natalie wrote in her note, "I'm not doing anything tomorrow. What do you say we get married?"

It was a small wedding, with only immediate family and a few close friends taking part in the ceremony. Natalie wore a form-fitting white lace gown with a cowl effect veil. A childhood friend, Barbara Gould, served as her maid of honor. R.J. picked his father as best man. Wagner, Sr., won a bet as soon as the ceremony was over. During his teens, R.J. had bet his dad he wouldn't marry before age thirty. He was twenty-seven when he married Natalie; she was nineteen. There was no mob scene of photographers or reporters attending the ceremony, only a studio cameraman who recorded the event. Scottsdale city marshalls patrolled the church area to keep out the uninvited.

The honeymoon got off to a bad start. The couple just missed the 5:00 P.M. Phoenix train that was supposed to take them to Chicago. They drove along the tracks, screaming and honking at the engineer. "Finally he saw us and stopped at an intersection. We scrambled aboard with sixteen pieces of luggage," Natalie said. Only one thing marred the festivities. R.J. had decided to let a friend of his come along on the train ride to take pictures of the whole thing. He did so believing his friend would honor their agreement that the photos were to be seen by no one but the newlyweds. The photographer betrayed them by selling the pictures to magazines. Natalie, who was already beginning to suffer emotionally from all the exposure, was devastated. This made R.J. even more enraged at his friend.

During their actual honeymoon, however, they knew nothing of the photo incident and managed to enjoy themselves tremendously. In a scene right out of a movie, R.J. carried Natalie over the threshold of their Chicago hotel suite. Once inside, it turned out the rooms were red and black, Natalie's favorite color scheme. It was no coincidence. R.J. had wired ahead and had the room redone to please her. After taking a train to Florida, they were supposed to spend five days on a lazy cruise around the Keys, but the rainy, cold weather prevented it. They headed for New York and some nightlife, but left after a few days. Too many people came up to them—taxi drivers, waiters, newsboys—wishing them well. They didn't mind being national celebrities, but they did want a private honeymoon. To ensure there were no more intrusions, they drove cross-country to Palm Springs and spent a week at the borrowed home of their friend Greg Bautzer. They saved the best for last. During their final honeymoon week, Natalie and

R.J. took his boat around the coast of Catalina. R.J. was at the helm and Natalie did the cooking. "What a gasser she is on a boat," R.J. told friends when the honeymoon was over.

They settled in R.J.'s Beverly Hills bachelor pad, and also into reality. Natalie had been under suspension from Warners for almost a year. R.J. had not made a movie in many months, too many months for an actor struggling to become a big name in Tinseltown. Finding the houses in Beverly Hills "so fantastically priced," they gave up looking and moved into Natalie's house in Laurel Canyon, and hunkered down for what they thought would be their inevitable rise to the top.

In quick succession, R.J. landed roles in *The Hunter* and *Say One for Me*. Natalie became very jealous. "I spent all my free time watching him work," she said at the time. "Because I've worked in pictures since I was a little girl, I feel more at home in a studio sound stage than I do in my own house. Sitting there watching R.J. perform is more nerve-wracking than when I'm in front of the camera myself. We go over his scripts together, and then I bite my nails as he goes through the paces. Sometimes," she added, "I caught myself acting out the parts with him. It must have looked awfully funny."

They were both keenly aware of the better-than-even odds that their marriage would not last. All Hollywood marriages, especially those between two stars on relatively equal footing, have a disastrously high failure rate. Those who cared to comment on the Wagner marriage—and what gossip monger wouldn't—gave it a year at the outside. This sort of thing can unnerve a married couple, make them feel extremely self-conscious. Compounding the problem for the stars are all those reporters who come right out and ask questions regarding the stability of the marriage and how each feels about the other's career. Natalie affirmed the constant presence of Hollywood's cynical eye: "When newspapers or magazine writers call for story material, they kind of hint around to find out how things are going. One columnist even asked me point blank if we'd be together for the next two weeks at least, as that was her deadline and she didn't want her story to come out wrong!"

Such needling can make a couple respond in ways, both public and private, that can be detrimental to the health of a marriage, especially if one star really does start doing considerably better than the other. This would not happen to Natalie and R.J. for a while. In the beginning, their marriage was blissful. They seemed to read each other's thoughts, and were delighted by what they read. Then, too, they were both strong-willed and willing to fight for their marriage. "I don't think you can go into marriage with a negative approach," said R.J. "We're not thinking of whether we can make it. We're going to make it and have fun at the same time."

"We're not expert on the subject of marriage," added Natalie, "but I think if we're left alone to work things out, we'll be just fine."

The Hunters was released the following year. As his portrayal of the smooth, swaggering, jive-talking fighter jock, R.J. got great reviews by any standard of measure and certainly the best reviews of his career so far. Among the critics, Irene Thirer wrote: "Robert Wagner never had it so good. . . . He gives a glib, flip performance . . . which, at last, stamps him as a player of distinction." It meant a lot to R.J.

But the actual audience response impressed him more. During the screening, members of the audience clapped loudly during his scenes. He was exultant. "It was as though I had finally arrived," he said. "All these years I've just been a young leading man, a juvenile. I got to be a star, at least in billing, pretty quick, but the studios always thought of me as the boy next door. You know, the smooth-talking and great-with-the-chicks type guy, but no actor."

Up until that point, R.J. had felt he had no place in Hollywood. "I played in pictures like *Prince Valiant*—a disaster, I looked liked Jane Wyman in that wig—*Beneath the 12-Mile Reef,* and *A Kiss Before Dying,* all of which were walk-throughs. Nothing. I could see my career was getting nowhere, but they kept renewing my contract and the fan mail kept coming in. But I still never felt I really had a career."

Ironically, when R.J. was sent the script for *The Hunters* he almost tore it up. "It was the usual kind of part for me, a one-dimensional boy," he said, "but the time had come to do something, so I told them if they wanted me to continue with those kind of parts, I didn't want to continue at the studio. I'd do the part only if they rewrote the character into a three-dimensional man." And rewrite it they did. R.J. was truly beginning to put his foot down and stand by his convictions.

"Now I figure I've served my apprenticeship," he continued. "I'm the last of the buildup boys to hit his stride. I started with Rock Hudson and Tony Curtis and they made it.

"I look at the kids coming along today and feel sorry for them. They're going to start as we did—with group lay-outs with other stars, then with actresses better known than they are, and then finally stories like 'What Does R.J. Think of Girls?' and that stuff. And then the mail will start pouring in and they'll be stars. But no one will ever take them seriously, just like no one ever took me seriously.

"During the first five years I was under contract at Fox, they'd just say, 'Report to such-and-such set tomorrow' and I'd clock in and draw my costume and get on with it. All I usually knew was the director's name. Sometimes not even that. And then there were always one or two kids who looked just like me. That, of course, was to show I was replaceable," he said.

If his bitter resentment of his treatment by Hollywood was clear before the release of *The Hunters,* what's equally clear is that soon after the release of his next picture, *In Love and War,* R.J. would speak very fondly of the "buildup" he got at Fox. Perhaps his tacit retraction of the indictment was due to his losing in his next couple of movies the professional ground he had gained with *The Hunters.* In addition, contract time was looming on the horizon. R.J. would insist on certain changes being made in the new contract, but he operated shrewdly. He didn't ask for them until he tried to assuage whatever ill feelings he might have incurred with his vituperative exclamations about what a bad deal he was getting.

Meanwhile, bolstered by his success, he gave all the credit for his graduation from the pretty-boy set to his marriage to Natalie: "But I was lucky. I got married and for the first time I began to see myself as a mature guy and I began to get confidence in myself, probably because there was someone else who cared whether I sank or swam.

"It was pretty wonderful hearing the audience applaud me, but the best compliment I got after the screening came when Natalie said: 'You know, R.J., for a while I thought you were somebody else.' Then I knew I'd broken the ice."

He was signed up for *In Love and War,* purely on the basis on what he'd done in *The Hunters.* As the cowardly Marine who works out his problems in battle, R.J. picked up mediocre reviews. But he still felt he was on his way. Marriage, the subtle partnership of love and careers that had raised R.J.'s and Natalie's hopes, was beginning to produce the pot of gold on schedule.

To relax, they took long trips on a boat that R.J. had owned since before their marriage. The yacht would help them get away from the peering eyes and nosy questions of reporters and fans. They would take as many trips as possible on it. Living constantly in the public eye was a wearying experience and this was their only recourse without actually going off to distant lands where "perhaps" they might not be recognized. The yacht smoothed the difficulties of their marriage and allowed the young couple to enjoy each other in peace.

It was only aboard the yacht, which R.J. jokingly named *My Other Woman,* that Natalie ever approached the idea of doing chores. "You should see her run our big boat," R.J. said, proud as he could be. "She looks so tiny that whenever we go to Catalina crowds gather round to watch her take up lines. We started our honeymoon on the boat." Natalie, to whom land-locked kitchens would forever remain uncharted seas, did the cooking on board.

"I'm the greatest when I'm on the boat. But I don't get near a stove at home. We have a little barbecue oven aboard, so I broil steaks and when we get out on the water we never want to come back."

They seemed as happy as two people could get. "I think we should have gotten married a long time ago," R.J. said at the time. "It's just wonderful. We have a manservant who cooks, cleans our clothes, and picks up after us and makes life easy, but don't think Natalie can't cook when she's on the boat. She can also run it, and she's a wonderful first mate. The boat is small and if we had a skipper it wouldn't be like getting away at all. We're going to buy a larger boat next year, because we both love fishing, swimming, and yachting."

One of the many rules they made for fostering and maintaining their happiness was the refusal to let their careers separate them. They served notice to the studios that neither would go on location unless the other could go along. They would not allow themselves to grow apart. "That usually comes from being separated for long periods," Natalie explained. "We got married to be together. We've seen too often what happens when people are parted for just a little while. It's a big danger, so why take the chance? I turned down a very good film role because it would have meant six weeks away from R.J. When I came to New York to make *Marjorie Morningstar,* R.J. came too. And when he had to work in Honolulu on *In Love and War,* I dropped everything to go along.

"It's not only separation of distance but separation of interests that we're guarding against," Natalie continued. "For example, we both agree on a goal and work together for it. That goes for little as well as big things.

"R.J. loves boats and I've come to love them, too. So we decided to invest in a boat as our 'home' and have a small house in town. That may not sound like much of a decision but we've seen lots of people in our position buy both a big boat and a big house, then end up nervous wrecks because of the money they owe."

Their decision on how to spend and save their money was a

predictably conservative and traditional one. At this point, 1959, their joint income was about $150,000 a year, but since R.J. was the head of the family, they decided to live on his income and either save Natalie's or use it for special luxuries. This method, certainly a sensible one if they could stick to it, had a great long-term goal as its motivating virtue. "Someday we want children," R.J. explained, "but we know that if we get used to living on both incomes we'll put off having a family because we'll have gotten in the habit of living too high. That has happened to too many other couples, and we don't want it to happen to us." Though reasonable in itself, this logic, examined closely, can reveal a certain hypersensitivity. There is perhaps just a little too much caution in R.J.'s words, so much caution that it exposes the marriage as admittedly fragile. "Handle with care" is written all over it, a sure invitation to an uncaring world to push a little harder and cause the whole thing to cave in. R.J. was not conscious of these ominous symptoms; indeed, he thought everything was going along quite beautifully. And at that point, it was.

For most of the marriage they preferred each other's company. "Clark Gable gave me the best advice I ever got," said R.J., explaining their stay-at-home nature. "He said the thing to do is go to the studio and do your job and then go straight home." In fact, R.J. and Natalie did spend a lot of time alone, just the two of them. One has to believe, however, that this had to do more with their genuine interest in each other than Gable's advice, albeit sound.

They banned home sittings with photographers and reporters. "We allow very few photographers in the house or on the boat because it's our home and it belongs to us," said R.J. "We see no need to share it with the public."

"When we were dating," Natalie recalled, "many of the things which most young couples in love cherish were spoiled for us. Once I was knitting an afghan blanket as a surprise gift for R.J.'s boat. Two days before I was to give it to him he learned of it in a gossip column. Another time, he bought me a beautiful ring as a gift but the jeweler tipped off a columnist and I read about it."

"We keep everything that is personal behind our own four walls," R.J. said. "Why should anyone else know what goes on in our home? Most people have their own lives and problems and they are probably a darn sight more interesting than the R.J. Wagners.'"

Finally, they would not exploit the fact of their being married to do roles together. "Will we never make a movie together?" R.J. asked rhetorically. "Well, if the parts call for it. Long ago," he continued, "we decided that marriage was not to be part of our careers but a part of our life. We plan to make films together but not if the script capitalizes on the fact that we are also man and wife." This would hold true, R.J. insisted, even for their newly formed production company, RONA, short for Robert and Natalie.

Semi-autonomy was their goal. Semi-autonomy from the studios. Semi-autonomy from the public. It was a goal that would become increasingly difficult to realize as the pressures of Hollywood and the vagaries of their careers continually distracted them from their purpose.

In late 1958, R.J. decided to tackle movie musicals as a way of enlarging his career possibilities. *Say One for Me,* starring Bing Crosby and Debbie Reynolds, was his first and only musical. R.J. turned out to be a fair song-and-dance man, but he had to work hard to do it. "I have been interested in singing and dancing for a long time," he said, "but strictly on an amateur basis. When it was decided that I would sing and dance in *Say One for Me,* I regarded it as a delightful challenge. But I sure got that gone feeling when I began to rehearse last November."

For one of the bigger numbers, R.J. rehearsed for weeks with chairs that were supposed to be the girls in the act. "I was pretty good with the chairs," he said. "But when the girls moved into the scene for the first time I found I had two left feet. But we worked it out, thanks to some expert instruction, and after the sequence was finally filmed those wonderful dolls presented me with a trophy cup."

Even Bing himself, who portrayed a priest in the film, seemed impressed by R.J.'s learning ability. "Bing's a wonderful guy, personally and to work with," R.J. said after the shooting was finished. But he still had to admit that song-and-dance wasn't the easiest side of the entertainment business. He called it "a rough racket, but fascinating. My regard for Fred Astaire and Gene Kelly has risen even higher than it was before." And he admired their earning power, joking that maybe he could get some of that big money in Las Vegas.

Despite his failure at musicals, he began another "scorn the studio buildup-system phase," knowing that it would soon be extinct. "Tony Curtis, Rock Hudson, and I were the last three guys to suffer through that," he said bitterly. "There'll be no more beefcake shots on Muscle Beach, no more sophomoric magazine interviews on romantic topics, or appearances in public with starlets. And like Tony and Rock, I'll say a fervent Amen. My wife Natalie adds her thanks, too."

Her career was recently back on track as well. Natalie had signed a renegotiated contract with Warners that upwardly adjusted her salary and allowed her to make several movies outside the studio every year. This is what R.J. wanted so badly, both for movies that he would appear in as well as for his interest in RONA. His contract with Fox didn't expire until the end of 1960, but R.J. was already planning the way he wanted the negotiations to go.

As soon as *Say One for Me* received lackluster reviews, R.J. began once again to soften his tune a bit with regard to the studio. At this point, he proclaimed himself a "star graduate" of the buildup system. By June 1959, he was giving the studio credit for his success. In a complete about-face with regard to his earlier statements about being a pretty-boy, he said, "Actors today are pushed on the public too fast. When I started at Twentieth-Fox,

Darryl Zanuck spotted me in small but important parts, so the public had a chance to get used to me.

"This is a different era in pictures than when I started ten years ago—in those days it was a pretty-boy era. Now everything is based on your record. And how can anyone create a record when pictures are so expensive that producers are afraid to take chances with new talent? For instance, in the old days, actors like Tony Franciosa and Brad Dillman would have been big stars at this stage of their careers," he said, as if to say that, given the chance, they "coulda been contenders," too.

"I could earn much more as an independent than I do on salary," he asserted, "but the studio is justified in benefiting from my contract. When the studio invests in a young prospect it is a gamble, an expensive one. After all, the studio's only incentive to build a star is the possibility of eventually having an expensive one in its films for only the price of his salary. The actor benefits from this system simply because there is no other way in which he could have prepared himself for stardom. Twentieth," R.J. concluded, "has given me more than ten years of experience; working with people like Spencer Tracy and Susan Hayward certainly helped me learn my trade." It was the all too familiar sound of gratitude that R.J. was trying to feed to the studios. It had gotten him this far, so why shouldn't it help him get the contract he wanted?

It was so painfully transparent though, so grasping in its display of need, that it easily revealed that R.J. was in an awkward situation. Why would a star who doesn't like the roles he's getting even consider continuing with his studio? Why would R.J. stay with Fox after he lashed out at the studio, saying its attitude—"We made you, but never forget: there are plenty of others"—was damaging?

Quite frankly, he stayed because he was newly married and afraid.

9

Gilded House

In order to give a semblance of stability to his life, R.J. decided to approach acting as if it were any other business. He spent several hours each morning dictating letters and ideas to his personal secretary, Nena Wills. He read the financial pages with a keen eye. He nosed around other studios to see what they were offering. With contract time imminent, R.J. became entrenched in his resolute desire to make his own decisions about parts and scripts. As usual, he sugarcoated his statements to the press and complimented his studio bosses about the career they'd given him. R.J. had other things on his mind as well.

In the fall of 1959, he and Natalie finally made the big move and bought themselves a house in Beverly Hills. It was a relatively modest English colonial, but it would not remain so for long. They were two very successful young people in the limelight of Hollywood and they wanted to have it all. As R.J. would later explain, "We tried to live like the glamorous movie stars of the past we had read about in movie magazines." They decided to redo the entire house in a Greek revival style.

Natalie thought she was capable of handling the job herself. Though she really had no basis for this belief, she launched into the project with tremendous enthusiasm. The renovation cost $150,000, a tremendous sum in 1959, took months to complete, and altered every aspect of the house. They probably could have just built what they wanted from scratch with a lot fewer headaches. But apparently they knew what they were about.

The remodeling included the installation of a swimming pool surrounded by Greek statuary and filled with "special salt water." Needless to say, it was the only one of its kind in the area. There was a six-foot-square marble bathtub, and intimate windowless bedrooms so that they could not be seen by prying eyes. Finally, an assortment of expensive antiques and valuable paintings completed the scene. Trying in vain to show some business sense, Natalie explained the reason for the super-costly furniture: "Our decorator, Dewey Spriegel, says that paintings and antiques are as good an investment as stocks and bonds." The floors were covered in white marble. Outside the house, they put up white columns. When the whole thing was finished it would be a dazzling white palace with details in gold.

Or so they thought. It was a disaster. After their marriage collapsed, the house remodeling not yet complete, it took almost two years to find a buyer for one of Hollywood's minor comic attractions.

Until that unhappy day, however, it was a blaze of glory for them. Natalie's bedroom alone must have been quite a spectacle. It was furnished with smoked mirrors, gilt walls, Louis Quatorze furniture, and a bedspread in green antique velvet. The adjacent dressing room, twenty feet by thirty feet, also had its own special charm. It was given a sunken Roman bathtub, with statuary swans spouting water. The bedroom and R.J.'s wood-paneled den alone cost $50,000. They moved in with only these two rooms ready, and the rebuilding went on around their heads.

In the midst of creating this white elephant, the Wagners also decided to buy a bigger boat. "We're without a boat, at the moment," R.J. told Hedda. "Sold it because we want a bigger one, a motor sailer, a fifty-five-footer with longer range." But they didn't want one like the one they had just sold. "A weekend as the guests of Claire Trevor and Milton Bren made us change our minds about owning another yacht. Milton is building his own boat just the way he wants it, so Nat and I have decided to do the same. We both love the water so much," R.J. concluded. The simple things just wouldn't do anymore.

"You know," reasoned Natalie to Louella, "it doesn't cost any more than taking long, expensive trips and we can have more fun traveling in our boat than flying anywhere in the world." Both Louella and Hedda took notice of just how much money the "young Wagners" must have been making. The young Wagners did not end up getting another boat until about eleven years later, when they weren't so young any more, but a lot wiser.

As the first few months of 1960 went by, the good times became fewer. Natalie had done a fairly good movie with James Garner, *Cash McCall,* and was getting some very good offers—offers of the kind of quality roles R.J. wanted so much for himself. One was for *Splendor in the Grass,* another for *West Side Story.* R.J. was getting offers too, but it was the same old matinee-idol stuff. He just could not accept he was that bad an actor, and turned them down. Natalie's offers required travel, and she decided she would go. Though, true to their agreement, R.J. would go along, these decisions were no longer being made in the spirit of marital concord. Natalie was growing away from the marriage, and R.J. was too busy thinking about his own slightly desperate situation to make the right conciliatory motions.

With hindsight, one could say that there was trouble on the horizon. Their agreement was heading for its biggest hurdle. Yet they still loved each other and were willing to work together to make the world believe that, unlike other Hollywood couples, they had suffered none of the symptoms of archetypal movie industry marriages. With one glaring exception: their addiction to talking with gossips.

Louella Parsons wrote in 1960:

> When pretty, slim, brown-eyed Natalie Wood and handsome Robert Wagner were married nearly three years ago, the cynics said, "We give this marriage a year, no more." A husband and a wife with

equally important careers are bound to be jealous if one gets better roles than the other.

Well, those dire prophets can eat their words. . . .

"Come on now, give the waiting world, especially all the newly-weds, your recipe for your blissful contented life," I said as [the Wagners] sat on the divan in my living room while we discussed our favorite subjects—sports and, of course, motion pictures.

"First of all you must have the same interests in life. I would say congeniality is the foundation for any happy married life," said Bob. "If you love each other, why would you be jealous of the career of the one you care for most?"

"On the contrary," interrupted Natalie, "I am just as much inter-ested in scripts Bob is discussing as I am in my own movies. You would be a pretty miserable person to turn green-eyed just because the one you love is getting a break."

"To show you how ridiculous even the thought of jealousy is in our lives, I never make a picture without asking Natalie to read the script and give me suggestions and her opinion on whether she thinks I should accept that particular story."

"And," said Natalie, "Bob always reads my scripts and I listen to his suggestions."

"Do you always accept his ideas?" I asked the gal with the dancing eyes and the doll-like face.

"No, we don't always agree, but at least we both respect each other's opinions."

If something doesn't quite ring true in all of this, it's because it's so hard to put on a front for the public, even when you have nothing to hide. In this case, it seems Louella tried to catch Natalie off guard a bit with her last question. Louella knew that no one's marriage was all fluffy love, as these two were pretending it was. With marriage, the harder you try to make it look good, the more likely it is there is something wrong, even if it has not yet actually surfaced. And Louella sensed that this something was very much in existence and tried to root it out. This must have been trying for the Wagners. But then, they had agreed to speak with Louella about their private life.

Their marriage, however, was strong enough for them to think that they could do something that all of Hollywood had wanted them to do for a long time: act together. Though they had never completely ruled it out, their plans to co-star in a movie took Hollywood by surprise. The newspapers were full of headlines such as "Wagner and Wood Break Pact." R.J. and Natalie tried to make light of the whole matter. This was a picture with roles worthy enough for both of them and yet the movie would not depend on them. It was the perfect compromise. "We didn't particularly want to make a picture together," R.J. told Hedda, "but when we read the script both parts were so good we couldn't pass it up. Many things offered us in the past had a good woman's part or a good one for the man; but if we'd co-starred in those, one or the other would have suffered. In this one we don't actually carry the romance. We marry different people."

"Most important," said Natalie, "we've got good parts in a good story. Now," she added, steering the conversation toward her flourishing career, "the good things all seem to come at the same time." And she went on to list five movies that she had been asked to do. R.J. could not do the same.

The movie they had decided to do, with "good parts in a good story," was called *All the Fine Young Cannibals*. It would be their only feature film together.

Cannibals, based on Rosamond Marshall's novel, *The Bixby Girls,* was supposed to be a controversial film. But because of the anxieties of the producers over some of the scenes, everything controversial ended up on the cutting room floor. The result was a melodramatic soap opera mishmash. A pretty farm girl, Natalie, and an amateur trumpet player, R.J., are in love but have no money—a far cry from their real-life problems. R.J. is a protégé of a blues singer, Pearl Bailey, who suffers throughout because her man has left her and married another woman. In the midst of his heartache at work, he gets Natalie pregnant. Not wanting to live in poverty for the rest of her life, she runs away to find a more secure life. Meeting a handsome, rich Yalie, George Hamilton, she captures his heart and marries him fast enough to have him believe that the baby is his, and then goes off to live the life of a rich housewife. R.J., in the meantime, gets his act together and becomes a famous night club musician and ends up marrying George Hamilton's sister. His wedding bells are to insure that he and Natalie will still be close.

Feeling confident about the picture, R.J. was very sure that this was just what he needed to get the contract he wanted. His mood, swinging up and down with dangerous rapidity, was again ebullient and swaggering. Would he and Natalie be willing to do television together, someone had the temerity to suggest. Responding brashly, R.J. said: "Sure we'll do television—if we can do it like Larry Olivier did it [in "The Moon and Sixpence"] with a superb writer and a director like Mulligan [Robert Mulligan, *To Kill a Mockingbird, Summer of '42*]. Sure, we'd do it. There should be more of that sort of thing on television. Our careers? Great! For both of us. For Nat, it's always zinged. But me—it took twelve years for me to convince them I was more than just a pretty boy."

The critics hated *Cannibals* and both R.J. and Natalie's performances, with good reason. They didn't act so much as pose. Unfortunately, this had been true of too many of R.J.'s performances, something he had not yet realized.

Thinking that he was much better than he was, R.J. entered into negotiations with Fox. Getting the contract he wanted, he thought, would be a small battle, but he was confident that he'd win them over in the end.

In August of 1960, the news came out that R.J. was ending his long association with 20th Century-Fox. Prognosticators were only surprised that he hadn't given in to the studio's demands. Other than that, it was no surprise that he came out the loser. R.J., they knew, had a completely unrealistic view of his acting abilities.

One day he would prove to the world that he was more than just a pretty face, but for now, all the studio could judge him from were some very dubious roles. They gave no proof R.J. could be trusted with major roles in serious movies. On the contrary, except for *Broken Lance* and *The Hunters,* his serious roles had basically all been flops. He did not look mature enough, his handsomeness was stamped with too much of the pretty boy, and his performances gave the feeling that he was none too bright. His innate intelligence didn't come through in his acting.

Fox didn't mind having him aboard as long as he conformed to this general view and did not make waves. R.J. couldn't accept this. Spyros Skouras, president of Fox, couldn't understand why. "What the hell are you beefing about," he demanded to know. "You're getting two thousand a week and working. There are hundreds of kids out there doing nothing." And he was right. "If you don't sign," Skouras said, "you'll never work again."

R.J. left the meeting. He went off to save his disintegrating career his own way. Skouras was wrong; the world was wrong. He *could* have a better career.

═══10═══

The Bride Wore Black

Putting on his best face, R.J. went off with Natalie to New York while she filmed *Splendor in the Grass*. He was thirty years old and starting his life over. If he was bitter, he tried hard not show it as he talked about his former employers: "They were good to me," R.J. said magnanimously. "I learned a lot and now I have to make my own decisions about parts and scripts. That's a problem," he added quickly. "If an actor makes a couple of flops he's in trouble. But there are plenty of people around to help." Even though he wouldn't admit it, R.J. was troubled, so troubled that at Natalie's urging he was seeing a psychiatrist.

R.J. had his heart set on doing *The Hustler*. "It's a great story," he said, "and it appeals to me particularly because I used to be a hustler myself." Hardly the thing one would expect from the son of a well-to-do steel executive. "I always could use the extra money," he said, "and anyway, all sorts of people used to be pool hustlers. The man who wrote the book—he's a college professor —was one. And I used to hustle at golf, too. That's a great game for hustlers." Since he once even scored a hole in one, R.J. probably made a lot of money in that trade. Unhappily for him, neither role panned out. Paul Newman got the part in *The Hustler,* which became a classic thanks to a priceless performance by Jackie Gleason as Minnesota Fats. Newman would make it up to R.J. in the future, saving him from one of his severest slumps by getting him a role in *Harper.*

In the midst of doing *Splendor,* Natalie decided to stay on in

New York and do *West Side Story.* Imagine R.J.'s sense of isolation. It even came through when he told a reporter about their immediate plans. "We were going to take a slow boat home, following completion of Natalie's work in *Splendor in the Grass.* It would take ten days, via the Panama Canal, and it would have been relaxing for Natalie. But she signed for *West Side Story* and now she'll have about ten minutes between pictures." When the news came, R.J. was just in the middle of negotiating for a forty-foot sailing boat. The plans to have one built had fallen through. It required too much attention and at this juncture of his life R.J. did not have the time.

Natalie's work forced him to cancel his plans. Ironically, this was probably the time in his life he most needed the solace of the ocean. "There is nothing like sailing," he mused. "One of the eeriest feelings is when there is no wind and the sea is calm. You just sit there and you can't do a thing. It feels like something will erupt from the sea. It's wonderful therapy. Natalie loves it, too. This is a terrific way to get away from the everyday things. Occasionally we have noticed that we haven't talked about pictures or roles or anything but the problems of sailing." A more apt metaphor for the state of R.J.'s career and marriage in 1960 would be hard to imagine.

Unbeknownst to fan magazines, teendom's most beloved duo found themselves struggling to get along. Nothing was working. No one was calling R.J. with good movie scripts; he was just sitting and waiting. It was all going down the drain. How long would it be before he and Natalie would have to go up against a Louella or Hedda again and answer all those prying questions? They could not pull it off now as they had in the past.

The marriage, originally designed with upward progression as the binding adhesive, had a fatal flaw: there was no contingency plan for one partner's not being able to contribute. This was a marriage founded on the principle of mutual success, with the male taking center stage. It was not a marriage where one party could stay home on sabbatical and close the door to the outside world while the other went ahead. They had not yet conquered the highest peaks. And it was only at the top that these two could stop striving, bound as they were by their love on the inside and their careers on the outside. Each was equally important to the relationship, and the worst of it was, the world knew it. How could they face the world now? How could they face themselves? It was a disappointment for both of them. Their beautiful duet was in terrible danger. The surreptitious storm clouds were gathering in the Wagner home, and the problems of sailing through the bad weather would indeed be the only topic of conversation.

Natalie was not one to stay with a sinking ship. She was already making headlines all over America by allowing Warren Beatty, her co-star in *Splendor,* to court her openly for the whole world to see. Even worse, R.J. was very often on the set. Perhaps R.J. didn't take it seriously—there was always somebody putting his arm around Natalie. Anyway, he didn't react with jealousy. One can only wonder if R.J.'s career problems were the cause of Natalie's marital infidelity. Natalie was an extremely faithful wife, the product of a strict Russian family, and marriage meant a lot to her. It was no light thing for her to have an affair. At this point in her life, however, stardom was more important to Natalie even than marriage. Her affair with Beatty was a necessary expression of that stardom. Much to R.J.'s chagrin, Beatty was there for Natalie at a time when she needed someone to fill that role; certainly, Warren Beatty is the worst person to have around a marriage on the rocks.

When they returned to Hollywood, R.J. and Natalie had only one thing in common: their address. Even though they still spoke to reporters about their plans for RONA Production Company and such, this was less frequently, and the press noticed a certain coolness between them. At home there wasn't any harmonious talk at all; Natalie was getting sharp-tongued and R.J. was brooding. He quickly got a role in *Sail a Crooked Ship,* another B-movie vehicle of the type he so despised. It flopped completely. The fact that he had been recently named to the best dressed list by the

Men's Apparel Club of California was no consolation. In fact, it only intensified his low self-esteem. He was a mannequin, nothing more.

R.J. could sense that a change of scenery was in order. He needed someplace where he could gain good experience and get away from being automatically type-cast for pretty-boy roles. As he began to explore the possibilities, it became evident that Natalie was unwilling to explore them with him. Was it not possible for him to stick it out in Hollywood? After all, she was doing fantastically well; that should be a consideration. The fact that these ideas were beginning to be aired was a strong sign that, at the most fundamental level of the marriage, their set of strict traditional values was being eroded by the exigencies of their careers.

Once they acknowledged the reality that their career aspirations were more important than the structure of the marriage, all the bonds quickly started breaking. The very reason for the marriage no longer existed. Still, each tried to pull the other back. After all, pure love, the last bond, is very obtuse when it comes to logic. The pulling would last for months. Finally, it could go on no longer. Besides, Beatty was still very much a figure in Natalie's life. It may have been this, in the end, that was the last straw.

R.J. came home one evening after finishing up for the day on the set of *Sail a Crooked Ship* and a terrific fight ensued. No one knows why it should have been this particular night at the end of June 1961, but the next day all of Hollywood was tittering with the news of the argument. "Did you hear that R.J. stormed out of the house to go stay with friends in La Jolla?" neighbors said. "Well, now those two are filing for a separation." The joint statement released by their press representative tersely said: "There is no immediate plan for divorce. Both are hopeful problems between them can be worked out."

The insiders felt it was not to be, and generally agreed that R.J. was the one being ousted. "Nat just got bored with him. She was the dominant one in that marriage. Bob's just an easygoing boy," said one friend. And elsewhere: "Female stars need conflict and

dominance from their husbands, even physical combat, and Bob
didn't give Nat anything like that." He would have crushed her
if he had: R.J. was a full foot taller and eighty pounds heavier than
Natalie. Anyway, it had nothing to do with that. Somehow, Natalie had managed to hurt R.J. deeply that night. Family and friends
said that Natalie always claimed R.J. had not been the villain in
the split-up. For a dramatic and tempermental young star like
Natalie, this was an uncharacteristic position to take.

R.J. was inconsolable. As far as he was concerned, it was time
to channel his concentration completely into his career. The tragedy was that his career was dead in the water, and would remain
so for many months. In the meantime, he continued to ponder
where he might go to gain new experience in different roles.
Europe offered the most possibilities. Once he'd made up his mind
to go, there was no turning back. The few times he and Natalie
talked, she could not convince him otherwise.

On April 27, 1962, Natalie finally filed for a divorce. Since she
was leaving for the Cannes Film Festival, which she'd attend with
Beatty, the filing was moved up and she managed to get her court
appearence in ten days. She dressed seductively, but as if she were
in mourning, totally in black—black hat, black silk suit, black
stockings, and black shoes. As usual, she had her way with the
judge and was granted her freedom in eleven minutes flat. Her
appeal was based on mental cruelty; she was a golf widow, she
said. Testifying before the court, she did not cry but her eyes
reddened noticeably. "The last year of our marriage," she said,
"Mr. Wagner preferred to be off by himself. He was always telling
me he was going out to play golf and didn't have time to discuss
our problems. . . . He said he didn't want to be married, that he
wanted to live in Europe, make it his permanent home. . . . I
became extremely upset and lost a lot of weight. I had to be placed
under a doctor's care." Later Natalie claimed to have lost ten
pounds from her normal weight of ninety-eight pounds.

Natalie's mother corroborated her testimony. "Mr. Wagner
was even rude to me and he even left Natalie alone when she was

sick with the flu." While Natalie was in the courtroom, her secretary, Mart Crowley, was packing her bags. Crowley had worked for the Wagners ever since he met them on the set of *Splendor in the Grass.* He felt torn by the divorce, loyal to both Natalie and R.J.

R.J. was out of the country during the proceedings. In late 1961, he'd left for England to shoot *The War Lover.* During his absence, one reporter denigrated R.J. by noting that Natalie's ex-husband "has been regularly described for ten years now as a 'rising young actor.' "

The perfect marriage had ended. Romantics everywhere mourned the demise of their symbol of eternal love. It was not a hate-filled ending, though; it had more to do with pride and the desire to succeed. With R.J. and Natalie unable to achieve their all-consuming goals on the same schedule, they couldn't go on together. Anyway, they were stubborn. R.J. would not allow himself to be cut off from his ideas about how to gain more respect as an actor, and Natalie would not allow herself to be cut off from the place where she was succeeding brilliantly. Both of them knew these were the real reasons for their divorce. R.J. and Natalie were reasonable enough not to let the event become an obsession.

At first, it was very hard for R.J. to accept the failure of his marriage. He looked at it as a consequence of the failure of his career. Soon enough, however, he was able to speak quite truthfully and frankly. "We were very vulnerable," he said. "The odds against a happy marriage in Hollywood are tremendous." R.J. was not trying to make light of the failed marriage. Under the circumstances, he was actually fortunate to come out of it relatively unscathed. For him and Natalie as well, there were no important bridges burned, no messy scenes. In fact, he blamed the constant, penetrating public gaze for the demise of his marriage. In a sense, he was right.

=11=
Roman Holiday

R.J. walked out on a million-dollar contract at Fox to work in Europe, but in his view, it was the best money he ever lost. He was learning to relax at long last, and he was working steadily.

The War Lover, a probing character study of a reckless pilot, turned out to be a good break for him. Though lacking a good script, the movie was intended to be serious and thoughtful. And when it was released, it was a success with the critics. Only the accidental death of R.J.'s stunt double in a parachute jump over the English Channel marred the good feelings that the movie's critical welcome inspired.

R.J.'s temporary break from Hollywood began a long transition period in his life. For six years, he would struggle to gain that threshold of success where an actor can take command of his life and control both the quality and the kind of professional appearances he makes. Finally, R.J. would find himself and his true calling when he relented to requests by agents and producers, some of whom had been pestering him with TV ideas for years, to consider "It Takes a Thief." Until then, R.J.'s life was marked by many highs and just as many lows.

In the course of his struggle to save his career, R.J. was to be just as involved in the task of resurrecting his confidence. To R.J., who for so many years had done the bidding of others, it would be a time to rediscover his real personality, suppressed for so many years. This would be no small matter. Instinctively, he believed that the unburdening of his soul would finally free him to be able to follow Spencer Tracy's advice. "Be natural," Spence had admonished, "be yourself." So far, that ability had eluded him. At this point, R.J. believed his career depended on how closely he could come to following that advice. More important, he knew deep inside that his happiness was contingent on doing something because he wanted to do it and not just because it pleased someone else. In the end, he would find his niche.

In exploring R.J.'s life, it's impossible not to be impressed by how hard working and earnest he is, even when selling himself. These qualities have always brought him back from the brink of disaster. It's not too much to say that these two elements of his character saved him from complete failure.

In 1961, they also saved him from the clutches of Joan Collins. The English sexpot, who had just broken off her relationship with Warren Beatty, made an attempt to woo R.J. while he was on her turf. But her hatred of Natalie for winning Beatty got in the way. Earnestly, R.J. told her he couldn't endure her mean words for his ex-wife, and the close friendship fizzled.

R.J.'s search to find himself brought him to Rome. In addition to the opportunity to work with stellar actors including Fredric March, Maximilian Schell, and Sophia Loren in *The Condemned of Altona,* the biggest draw of all in Rome was the director Vittorio de Sica. Years later, R.J. explained why he went. "I took a salary cut to do [the film] because I knew I'd learn, and I did learn," he said.

From the first moment he entered the business, R.J. was always trying to learn, whether to impress others or to feed himself when he sensed something lacking in his ability to perform. Was this quest for learning somehow symptomatic of R.J.'s central dilemma, his quest to become a great actor? You can't learn to be a great actor unless the talent is there, just as you can't raise a plant from ground where no seed has been sewn. You can't become a great musician if you don't have a great ear that can be developed. R.J. has a good ear and he is a good actor. When expertly directed, he has always been a good actor. As he himself said in the mid-sixties, "As far back as *With a Song in My Heart,* I was pretty damn good." And he was. But very rarely has he been great.

In that regard, his attempts to "learn" were in vain. On the other hand, R.J.'s ability to work hard and his desire to be himself —more easily achieved than greatness—made those learning times valuable. By the end of the transition period, he had uncovered that now unmistakable personality of urbanity, trustworthiness, and suave sophistication that is as interesting as it is charming and beguiling. This is the R.J. we have come to know and love on television. And even more wonderful, it's his real personality.

In Rome, he exercised his sophistication, sitting at the cafés along the Via Veneto, reflecting, posing as only the Romans can do. Had he arrived only days earlier, his composure would have been threatened. There on the Via Veneto sipping expresso, he would have run into Natalie and Warren Beatty, fresh from their triumph at Cannes. Thankfully, he missed running into them. After a few days of relaxation, R.J. began work on *The Condemned of Altona,* based on Sartre's play about a wealthy shipping family that, for the sake of lining its pockets, caters to a succession of German governments, including the Third Reich.

"The night before I was to do my first scene with de Sica," he recalled, "I became physically sick with nerves. Then in the morning I saw Freddie March's hands were shaking too and I thought: 'God, if he's nervous with all his experience, what am I worried about?' I felt better after that. But you can't imagine what it was like for me to be working in Europe after twelve years in Hollywood. I'm not knocking the place—after all, I grew up there. But it's a different world.

"One of the troubles with Hollywood is that no one tells the truth. Every time I complained I was getting nowhere they'd say: 'But kid, you're great. We just saw your rushes. Just great.'

"Of course, I wasn't the only one. Rock Hudson had the same

battle. So did Tony Curtis. They all sneered at Tony, a little Jewish kid from the Lower East Side, because he was always trying to improve himself.

"But breaking away isn't easy. The money's coming in but you're always living above your income. So you're crippled. You're insecure too, for Hollywood is an insecure town.

"Natalie and I used to send out a hundred and fifty gifts—heaven help you if you forgot someone. Booze for the studio cops, presents for all the telephone girls. There was no end to it. On top of that, we sent out seven hundred and fifty Christmas cards. You daren't offend anyone.

"In the end, I was almost destroyed. So I refused a new contract. I quit. And for weeks the phone didn't ring. Nobody came knocking at my door. People keep saying I was insane to have done it."

Hollywood had become hell to R.J., and Rome was looking like paradise. Shooting *Altona,* R.J. enjoyed a unique working relationship with the director. And de Sica liked R.J. He decided to include R.J. in all aspects of the making and directing of the film. De Sica wanted to school R.J. in the elements of filmmaking that are termed "behind the camera," instead of R.J.'s usual purview in front. "[De Sica] really took me under his wing, let me work beside him in story conferences, and even in the cutting room." This was invaluable experience for an actor who wanted some day to produce his own movies. R.J. worked very hard alongside de Sica, and his apprenticeship paid off handsomely. Today R.J. is one of Hollywood's most successful producers, one who gives a damn about the quality of the product that reaches the screen.

Despite the excellent working conditions, *Altona* was very poorly received, and the reviews of R.J. were especially demoralizing. "This film is such a hopeless mess that it is difficult to know where to begin criticizing it," said British critic Tom Milne. Other critics said that as the decent-minded but weak son, R.J. was out of his depth. His own description of the part sounded like a description of himself in the worst days. "I played a weak and controlled son whose life was a series of capitulations," he said knowingly.

The bad notices on *Altona* didn't bother him, however, since he had tackled the film purely for the purpose of gaining valuable experience. R.J. spared his emotions many times with this attitude. It's a good attitude to have, but one that requires enormous mental fortitude. R.J.'s conviction that he could act and act well was strong enough for him to be able to achieve that level of detachment where emotional strains are eased by rationalization. This allowed him to go on. Part of his self-control came from the time he was spending in therapy, which he'd continued even after his marriage collapsed and Natalie was no longer there to urge him to the psychiatrist's couch. *Altona*'s bad reviews, however, were not without a silver lining. He decided their tone was different from the kind of reviews he'd received in the past; for once, the critics seemed to accept him as a professional. For R.J., this shift was a monumental stepping-stone, one that he felt opened the door to the movie roles he had been fighting for.

While in Europe, R.J. also played in *The Longest Day,* a Zanuck extravaganza about the D-Day invasion. In his free time he continued to do as the Romans do, drinking cappuccino at La Tazza D'Oro and returning again and again to the Via Veneto.

And in the small cafés around Cinecitta frequented by the Roman film circles, R.J. met the woman who would become his second wife.

An erstwhile actress who, like R.J., was thirty-two years old, Marion Marshall had been his friend back in the early days at Fox. Now twice divorced, the second time from director Stanley Donen, she had two sons in her custody. Strong-minded and cool-headed, Marion knew her likes and dislikes and made no apologies for the things she preferred. She liked R.J., and sought to teach him that he had nothing to fear from his past. She was out to prove that with continued effort, he had it in him to achieve the independence he had lost in his desire to succeed. At a time when R.J. was suffering through tremendous bouts of self-doubt and was struggling to suppress an inferiority complex, Marion's calm, reassuring nature was an oasis from whose well he could drink confidence. There was also an extremely pragmatic reason R.J. became so involved: he never much liked being alone.

They became engaged, but since R.J.'s divorce from Natalie would not become final until April 1963, he and Marion would have to wait until then before going ahead with their plans for marriage.

Returning briefly to the States in early 1963 for film story conferences, R.J. was full of hope for the future and very candid about his past. It was a time to start putting his life in perspective. He emphatically denied that his leaving Hollywood for Europe had anything to do with his breakup with Natalie and maintained that he didn't carry a torch all the way to England. "I had those commitments before Natalie and I ever broke up. I guess you could say I fled the shallowness of Hollywood life. I was having personal problems as well as career problems. Nobody was beating my door down wanting me in films. It wasn't that I couldn't get work. It was that I couldn't make people think of me in a different type of casting from the typical program picture.

"I didn't want a beachball in my hand," R.J. continued, explaining his disaffection for Hollywood at that time. "But understand this, that doesn't have anything to do with Hollywood. It has to do with me. I started in this town when I was eighteen years old. And after twelve years people take you for granted.

"There comes a time in everyone's life when you get hungry," he said. "And I don't mean for food or money. I mean in terms of what you want to do. It's easy to play it safe. I could have done a television series or other movies, but they weren't the kinds of things I wanted. I wanted to progress as an actor." Those who knew him could sense his enthusiasm for the kind of commitments he was making to his craft. He talked very excitedly about his work with de Sica and his desire to get back to the States on a permanent basis to work on some interesting new projects. He felt his efforts in Europe had given his career "traction" and that he had solved some of his professional problems.

Before his second marriage, R.J. and Marion traveled to Scottsdale to visit Bob and Chat Wagner so that R.J. could introduce his fiancée to her future in-laws. After this Arizona respite, they went back east for several months to live it up in New York.

Finally, on July 22, three months after his divorce from Natalie became final, R.J. and Marion were married. The civil ceremony took place at the Bronx County Courthouse in New York City, with a state supreme court justice officiating. The newlyweds then headed back to Rome, where R.J. fulfilled some contractual obligations.

Though not yet enjoying the career he wanted, R.J. didn't lack the necessary funds to enjoy himself and pamper Marion with lots of material items, including great sports cars. They had Alfa-Romeos, Lancias, Jaguars, and a Bentley. They became notorious throughout Rome for the number of cars that were stolen from them. Although the Bentley attracted much attention from kids playing in the streets, it was never stolen. All the other cars were taken, some of them twice. The thieves were usually burglars looking for a fast getaway. One burglar, who, it was found out later, had committed 192 burglaries, totaled Marion's Lancia in a chase. "He used it to do a job," Marion said, obviously amused. "The cops saw him. He jumped in my car. He was doing a hundred and ten kilometers when he hit four other cars—in my Lancia." Dealing with the Italian police in these situations can be an infuriating tango with red tape, as R.J. found out. "Bob was lucky to get out of the place in two days." Marion laughed, her own experience being much less taxing. "He just went from bureau to bureau, all over the place. You're luckier if you're a pretty girl. And be sure to dress up. Wear your diamonds. Don't go to the police looking poor. They fall all over themselves." R.J. tried all sorts of gadgets to try to thwart the thieves, but they never worked. The cars still got stolen.

But he still loved the Romans. "They're wonderful," he said.

They found him simpatico as well—he'd learned their language. Throughout Europe, R.J. was treated with respect. Here comes Robert Wagner, the locals would say, we hear he's doing good things.

But R.J. wanted to get back to Hollywood and hear the same thing in English.

12

Getting By With a Little Help From His Friends

Coming home to the States, R.J. sensed his time had come. He felt he'd done what he had to in order to break out of the stereotypical boy-next-door mold and had finally earned credibility as an actor. He'd worked with de Sica, and that great director had encouraged him to be part of the decision-making process. R.J. believed he'd grown with this experience and that he should now be taken more seriously.

As far as his personality was concerned, he'd matured. Not to the point where he couldn't play the occasional practical joke on the set, occasionally telling new crew members that when he touched his ear, it was the sign to leave the set. Of course, he always made sure that efforts to stay within schedule were never disrupted and that no one was hurt. He still liked to gamble, play sports and sail, and he was always trying to learn as much as possible. "I'm trying to improve myself always," he would say when asked why he read so much. His Harvard Classics were well thumbed. But now R.J. was less apt to try to please others unless it pleased him to do so. Naturally, he was always polite. This was his trademark. But he no longer bent over backwards to accomodate what he felt was an unfair request. Slowly, his performances began to reflect his own suave and agreeable personality. But he wasn't yet comfortable with relying on himself while playing a role. Still, the critics were finally in positive agreement. For the first time, they all liked a performance, in *The Pink Panther*.

During the filming of the first in a series of Inspector Clouseau farces, R.J. became a father. He was thirty-four. Katharine (Kate) Wagner was born on May 12, 1964.

Although he relished the added responsibility, he still felt rather young in his professional life. Years later, R.J. recalled some of the problems he had on the set of *The Pink Panther,* problems that were symptomatic of the uneasiness he felt toward his career. "I was full of fear," he admitted. "I remember Peter Sellers saying, 'What the hell are you doing with your eyes?' I was hooding them, you see, because I was so scared of the camera. And that was a long time after I'd started acting."

The tone of these few sentences, spoken by R.J. more than fifteen years after the shooting of *Panther,* is striking in the way it compares to his earlier utterances. There's a sense a confidence here, an acceptance of the self that fairly overpowers. This was the serenity of mind R.J. was seeking to achieve in 1964. It would be years before he would feel comfortable enough to substitute his real feelings for the glib remarks that he used to shield himself from the prying eyes of the public.

Not only did R.J. get raves, but *The Pink Panther* was extremely well received, which made it a double boon for R.J. to be a part of the production. The movie was a smash success, and R.J. formed a lasting friendship with co-star David Niven. But after *Panther* was done, R.J. was astounded to find that he was not in demand for other good roles. He waited and he waited, but the phone just didn't ring. The only consolation was that he could spend a lot of time with his family.

As the months went by, R.J. began to get desperate. Was he ever going to work again? What a strange time to have your career come to an end, he thought, after a big hit in a popular movie, when you're still in your mid-thirties, and with a daughter just born. The idea of it was frightening.

Enter Paul Newman. He was getting ready to do *Harper,* a movie about a fading gumshoe cajoled into the intrigues of a rich, corrupt family whose patriarch has mysteriously disappeared. Harper's task is to find the missing man, although it becomes quite evident that many in the family don't want him found. Among the entourage is the missing man's neurotic pilot. Newman wanted R.J. for that part. Producers, agents, hairdressers, all Hollywood thought Newman's choice was lousy, but he persisted. "It wasn't easy," R.J. recalled. "Jack Warner and I have never been friendly, and he was determined that I not be in *Harper.* Paul felt otherwise and prevailed. Thank God Paul is quite formidable when he's on your side. You know what I did for two whole years before I made *Harper?* I sat on my behind in this town praying for work. I finally worked, thanks to Paul." The Newmans and R.J. have been friends ever since.

To say that *Harper* raised R.J.'s spirits is an understatement. He was so overjoyed by the real success he had in the role that friends could practically feel it when he entered a room. In the words of great jazz legends, he was hot, and he knew it. Walking into a restaurant to have an interview with Sheilah Graham, he fairly skipped along, gravity having temporarily lost its grip on him. He was considering TV. Blake Edwards was creating a show just for him about "the man who has everything." R.J. thought he fit the bill, though he worried that his style was too subtle for TV. "I would have to react within the situation, not over it," he said in actors' lingo.

During that interview, he veered from one subject to the next in a manic kind of high. He was living in Tarzana, a suburb of Los Angeles that had once been part of the estate of Edgar Rice Burroughs, author of the Tarzan books. Burglars had been invading the area, and R.J. didn't like it and he wanted it stopped. He talked about it with Miss Graham at length. There was no holding R.J. back. He was on a roll.

He wanted to mold a racehorse, he said. He was living. He did not have a care in the world. But he would get serious about his treks to Europe. "It's difficult to talk about Europe because people accuse you of being anti-American. But there is nothing like being in a country as a foreigner. I would like to live there but I can't always arrange my work," he said. This was certainly a switch from the man who had wanted to come back to Hollywood two years earlier.

As they say, don't wish for something because you might get it. As has happened before and since, the Blake Edwards TV series died before it got off the ground, and R.J. was signed to do another movie in Italy, *The Biggest Bundle of Them All,* with Raquel Welch. Things could have been worse. Although a light comedy, this was a movie where R.J. would be expected to act. One of his co-stars, moreover, was Vittorio de Sica. R.J. would go into any project with this man. "It's the best part I've had in a long time," he said, radiating enthusiasm, "not to mention an excuse to get back to Rome." Besides, Universal had signed R.J. to a contract that was very much to his liking. It included an innovative career program that R.J. felt encouraged "people who want to do good work." It was the sort of thing he had been looking for at Fox five years earlier. R.J. had indeed gained ground.

Before going to Europe, he filmed *Banning,* with Anjanette Comer, Jill St. John, Guy Stockwell, and James Farentino, about the corruption in and around a posh L.A. golf club. R.J. played the title role, a semi-pro whose career is ruined when he's slandered by a dishonest pro, Stockwell. Comer is having an affair with Stockwell and Jill St. John hankers after R.J. Nearly twenty years later, that last scene would play itself out in real life.

13

Coming Out From Under the Cover

The Biggest Bundle of Them All, a slapdash adventure movie about a fumbling group of criminals out to kidnap an American gangster, had a good cast going for it, including Edward G. Robinson, Godfrey Cambridge, Vittorio de Sica, and sex symbol Raquel Welch, but the critics were nonplussed by the results. But a light comedy movie should never be taken too seriously and, for sheer fun and excitement with a dash of romance, *The Biggest Bundle of Them All* was well worth the price of admission. R.J., as the debonair but concerned leader of the motley crew, is in his element. The inspired casting here later influenced "It Takes a Thief" producers to cast him as their lead.

A staff assistant on "It Takes a Thief" pointed out R.J.'s appeal a couple of years later. "Whatever the cover," he said, "there's always that same suaveness, the good looks, the charm. He's a great ladies' man, on the show that is." More than that, his adventure-role portrayals are the quintessence of international chic laced with a touch of humor, very much à la David Niven. R.J., though, is more athletic and hence more capable looking than his late friend. This is what makes R.J. so unique. His very presence on camera signals to the viewer's inner self a world of glamour, adventure, and high jinks, and the ability to get away with it all. The passport of sophistication is better than diplomatic immunity, which disqualifies one from excitement.

He may have been on a high, but Raquel Welch still upstaged R.J. in Europe. Her fabulous bod was gracing every European magazine and everyone wanted to see more of her. "I've never seen anything like the deluge of photographs of Raquel in the European magazines," R.J. said. "She was getting a hundred and fifty thousand a picture before anyone saw a foot of film on her." Was R.J. jealous of Raquel's good fortune? It's very doubtful, since money was never R.J.'s problem. What distinguishes R.J. from most actors are his desires: a home, a family, a flourishing and respectable career; things money can't buy.

Because of Raquel's notoriety, however, she could be somewhat dictatorial on the set of *The Biggest Bundle of Them All.* "At the start of rehearsal she was full of suggestions, and if we'd gone along with them she'd have ended up playing my part," R.J. said. After the movie was finished and R.J. was back in the States, he explained with his usual magnanimity that it was mostly zeal that drove Raquel and that he and de Sica had been able to handle the situation without bending any egos. R.J. has always been a considerate person, and he's always been a team player, never letting down the production. His sincerity, though, was becoming a little less forced. He was beginning to feel he didn't have to be sincere, and this made him doubly so. "But I'll say this for [Raquel]: when Vittorio de Sica and I sat down and explained things to her, she got the point at once. She's highly intelligent and if she will learn to be less fierce in her approach to her career, I think she'll make it."

Considering his own fierce determination to star in high-quality roles, his statement proves he was changing. He was beginning to become a little more realistic about his own career. Perhaps at this point R.J. was starting to lose his obsession for the great roles. He was thirty-seven, and it was time to take stock of his life, to mellow and give thanks for the good fortune he was enjoying. His roles now were, if not terribly complex, at least three-dimensional. And he was in big demand to make more movies of this sort. R.J. began to feel he knew what he wanted, and his insecurity was diminishing as a result. "Bob's real life has been developing under cover," said a close friend at that time. "On the surface, he's strong, flashy, athletic. Under all the action and muscle, he's been shy, uncertain, withdrawn—a sweet guy with a lot of hang-ups. He was crushed by the failure of his marriage to Natalie Wood. He went to Europe for a while to think things out, about himself and his work. Ever since, he's been changing steadily. I think he's begun to come to grips with the things that were throwing him."

As a result, in late 1966, R.J. was working harder than ever. "I had a tough time when I first came back [from Europe]. I waited for something good and got it in *Harper,* with Paul Newman. I've done two television shows for Bob Hope's 'Chrysler Theatre.' Before that, *Mr. Roberts* in Chicago. I've just finished a pilot for ABC, 'It Takes a Thief,' about the biggest thief in the world." The years of transition, of searching for his proper place in the industry, were fast coming to an end.

Although R.J. didn't yet realize it, "It Takes a Thief" would show him how he could be his own boss and finally enjoy himself. The confidence that had been eluding him was just coming back and would be cemented in his psyche by his experiences in television. "It Takes a Thief" would lead him where he could be himself, polite but not diffident, engaging but not artificial. Soon, he would finally be at peace with himself.

14

Winning With More Than a Smile

True love is like a revelation, and like a revelation, changes the importance of everything that has come before. For R.J., that revelation would be in his finding a niche on the small screen. It wouldn't be a passionate love, but it would be right. He would never know that depth of feeling in TV that he dreamed of attaining in movies. But sometimes heavenly dreams must be sacrificed for the sake of earthly happiness.

Like all those who aim for the heights, R.J. was at first reluctant to "step down" into TV. Like a slumping major-league ballplayer who doesn't want to find out he's no good in the minors either, R.J. thought TV might be a bigger risk than staying where he was. "At first I was really hesitant. It was a gamble," he said, "and I won."

Though not necessarily slumping—in fact R.J. starred in a number of movies during the time he was making "It Takes a Thief"—he certainly didn't go into TV because he was looking for great acting opportunities. He did it to see if it might not be another way to become a household name. There's no doubt that R.J. was well known, but he had slid down from the prominence he'd known as a teen idol. At thirty-eight, he was still being called an "anonymous actor." Viewers couldn't quite place him. Regularly seen, he still could not boast a strong nationwide following. R.J. needed a boost, and TV was the perfect answer. He didn't know yet how perfect.

When "It Takes a Thief" hit the TV screens, all the newspapers started doing stories on him. Invariably, the reporters would have to acknowledge the five-year gap in his career. It was time-to-catch-up-with-R.J. time. "So," they would begin their stories, "what's with Robert Wagner, that nice young man who married Natalie Wood—what's he been doing lately? If ultimate success has not quite reached him, he has at least proved himself extremely durable." How else were they going to explain him?

His public, rather glitzy marriage to Natalie and his problems in Hollywood still made good copy. Bringing their readers up to date on these things was more important than finding out about "It Takes a Thief." Just another TV show, they thought. Probably going to be a flop.

R.J. didn't care. He was surprised to find that talking about failures was a cathartic experience. It was a way for him to get in front of his past professionally and to get over it emotionally. "Fox and Warner Bros., the two studios where I worked the most, did everything they could to make me great. And I simply wasn't," he admitted. "Well, I've learned." Gone was the feeling of resentment; in its place was the achievement of self-knowledge. "He's changing, growing," said Leslie Stevens, producer of "It Takes a Thief." "The realities around him, he's embracing them, he's not hiding from them or withdrawing from them. He's becoming more emotionally liberated. He's warmer, more charming than he was before, when he felt he *had* to be warm and charming."

With "It Takes a Thief," R.J. felt he'd graduated from the category of "rising young actor" to that of consummate Hollywood veteran. "I wouldn't do another film just for the sake of doing another film," he said. "I've had my experience in all those B-films. On occasion, Darryl Zanuck would yank me out for a cameo in a better film, and at the time, it was important for me to be in films. Now it's not. I've had it too much the other way. I have too many other things to do now. I think I've had enough experience to know what I want." For the first time, people were beginning to realize more than a charming smile was responsible for R.J.'s durability.

R.J. had found in himself a style that came off very well on TV. It turned out to be very similar to his own personality. "His work as an actor is growing," producer Stevens continued. "He's been built up as a studio commodity, but he's adding in artistry, and he's sensitively dedicated to the work. Recently, he's discovered his ability to project himself, his real self. At one time, he was afraid to show himself. Now he's willing to be what he is, first and foremost—to stand or fall on that." This made R.J. infinitely more comfortable with his career. Now he was able to indulge his desire to be honest in all he did. When trying to be natural in his troubled early years, he had been anything but; now he was relaxed.

R.J.'s ease in front of the camera was one of the reasons why the movie *Winning,* made in 1969 with Paul Newman and Joanne Woodward, was such a success. Facetiously retitled by Woodward as "Cool Hand Luke Finds Rachel in the Sack With the Thief," the movie chronicles the lives of several race car drivers. Woodward is married to race car driver Newman, who has stiff competition from the weak but villainous R.J. The competition between the two drivers escalates throughout the picture and gets personal when R.J. and Woodward have an affair. But for the actors, the real fun "was learning how to drive a racing car," R.J. recalled. "It took us three months. We even were accepted by the Racing Association afterwards." For some of the most dramatic scenes, "film clips from a sixteen-car crash in 1967 were used," explained R.J. The movie demanded precision driving from the actors, as it had to be matched exactly with scenes from actual 500 races at the Indianapolis Speedway. Though R.J. drove 150 miles an hour in the movie, he was not as charmed by the fast lane as Newman was, who continues to race to this day.

The well-acted, trenchant scenes coupled with the very exciting racing episodes made for gripping drama. The critics loved it, as did the audiences.

R.J. continued to make movies after *Winning,* but since "It Takes a Thief," his attention has been more or less fixed on TV productions. At first it was a matter of survival. Since "It Takes a Thief," was such a risk in R.J.'s eyes, he became obsessed with turning out a success. However, he made no apologies for turning to TV. TV was his way of breaking the final barrier between his real self and his public image. "I was constantly doing what I thought should be done, according to what I thought people expected of me. I was always trying to satisfy others, to adjust to them, to avoid conflicts.

"Sometimes, I'd react as strongly in the other direction. I'd be defensive and angry. I remember once, in an airport, three years ago, someone beckoned to me with his finger. I dropped him. A perfect stranger, and I smashed him. I had the feeling he thought I'd jump at the gesture of a finger.

"The effect of all this concern with what other people expected of me—with the impression I was creating on them—was a loss of—well, I was locked up. I couldn't really see other people. I couldn't be seen myself. I wasn't even seeing myself. I was unable to communicate.

"It kept me from being happy, from getting any kind of contentment. And it affected my work." That R.J. was able to intellectualize his problems had a great deal to do with why he survived and came out a success. His wife, Marion, also had had a great deal to do with helping him overcome his fear of self-assertion. "Marion taught me how to control my own destiny," he said. "I started to believe in myself because she believed in me so much."

R.J. no longer relied on other people's judgments. He realized that being so heavily influenced by others could be a bad thing. This was the influence he and Natalie had tried to avoid when they shut their front door, but it had been waiting for them in the privacy of their thoughts. It was the influence of Hollywood that told a naïve boy not to question whether he wanted stardom. He listened for a while, but it damned him to years of gut-wrenching introspection. It was Louella, Hedda, and the other Hollywood icons that skewered his priorities.

"People," R.J. decided, "are constantly setting up false restrictions on you. Don't smoke, don't drink, don't make love, don't live! I'm trying to eliminate all these restrictions from my life. I'm much happier now. And I'm freer all the time, freer as a person and as an actor, free to be myself.

"You see, I want very much to be myself. I don't want to be locked up. I want to be visible. Everyone wants it, it's right to want it. I want to be simple, exposed, and seen."

As the Nielsen ratings for "It Takes a Thief" could attest, he was certainly being seen.

15

It Takes a Boldness

/ /I t Takes a Thief" was a high adventure-comedy of the first order about a prison inmate, Alexander Mundy (Wagner), who is paroled into the custody of Noah Bain (Malachi Throne), the head of a counterespionage organization, the SIA. Bain figures that since the spying game is in essence condoned larceny, the best at it are thieves. His motto is: To catch one, send another one after him. Mundy can't understand why he's been let out of prison, but when he finds himself the owner of a beautiful house with three gorgeous women as his assistants, he doesn't complain.

In the 1968 pilot, chock full of cameos by hot stars, Mundy fails his first assignment. Put under house arrest, he persuades his warden, one of the beautiful spy assistants, to help him try again. This time he succeeds, and is offered a job with the SIA. In the following episodes, he continues his dangerous missions, never failing to be surrounded by beautiful women. Liking the atmosphere, he becomes reformed, and one of the organization's top agents.

At first, "It Takes a Thief" was only supposed to be a made-for-TV movie. But then ABC bought it and decided to give the whole idea a shot as a series. "Iron Horse" was going off the air, and with the juggling of time slots it had in mind, the network had an hour of prime time going begging. In the rush to get the show ready, the producers chopped out all the cameos and the result was aired on Tuesday, January 9, 1968, as the first episode. After that it became an hour-long show. Though the critics decided it was a confused and derivative James Bondian hodgepodge of "The Man From UNCLE," "I Spy," and "Mission Impossible," and that it required good looks and good health more than acting ability, ABC went with the series.

The jibes may have hurt R.J., but he used them to try to improve the quality of the production. This he did with a vengeance. "You could say, the boy grew older," R.J. said, "and you'd be right. So right." Usually a night person, R.J. changed quickly. He went to bed at 11:00 P.M. and got up very early and went to the set. "I used to fly down to Los Angeles [from his home in Palm Springs]," he said, "but lost so much time getting clearance in bad weather that I took the car instead. It took an hour and forty-five minutes to two hours on the freeway, and if I got stuck in traffic, I could always get some work done, reading scripts or dictating." Commenting on the change of life-style, R.J. noted that it disciplined his eating habits, forcing him to drink less and eat more health foods. He didn't mind; he wanted the show to go on, whatever the cost. "I always felt the character would work. If it hadn't, people could have said that Wagner is just about finished." The pressure that R.J. was under impelled him to take over the set and eventually become the production's main catalyst. Though no longer under the same pressure, R.J. continues today to be unrelenting in his drive for excellence.

R.J. knew what he wanted. "He's much more confident than he used to be," said a friend of his at the time. "He takes a more definite stand in his own existence. He knows now where he's going and what he wants to do in the business." R.J. had good reason for wanting to keep the show on the air. Besides the following that he was building up, and the $10,000 per episode that he was making—astronomical for a TV star of that time—he was being treated like a king by the studio. A huge dressing room, his approval on publicity shots, and a limousine to ferry him wherever he went were just a few of the perquisites. Most important, he got to make most all the production decisions.

"The schedule seems to be the most important factor," he said, already sounding like a harried producer. "Most of the energy expended is in that direction—keeping up with the schedule. As a result, one has to fight like hell to get quality on the screen, and it isn't easy." Sometimes, the cast would not get the script until two hours before shooting.

Each segment of "It Takes a Thief" was supposed to be filmed in six days. That the first four episodes took seven did not bode well for relations with Universal Studios, where the series was being produced. But instead of trying to assuage the studio's anxieties about cost overruns, R.J. screamed for a day of rehearsal time. "One day of rehearsal would help," said R.J., "but they say we can't afford it. The wasted time we'd save by that day's rehearsal would more than make up for its cost, I believe. When I did the movie *Harper* with Paul Newman we rehearsed a whole month. Newman insisted on it." R.J. did what he had always done in these situations of conflict, he complained to the press. Some concessions were made. R.J. took more time when he thought it was needed, and nary a word was heard from the boss.

Another way time could be saved, R.J. argued, was if he could have the same crew. "A good dolly man and camera operator save a lot of time, especially when you don't have to explain to new ones each week what is wanted. Don't get me wrong now, I'm not blasting TV, but I'm saying these things make TV more difficult to do." R.J. may have been under pressure, but he was not scared to speak his mind. He was given the same crew on a permanent basis throughout the run of the series. He had learned that by putting his foot down he could lift the burden of anxiety from his shoulders and leave himself free to get the job done. "If you go in not believing in what you're doing, you've just got to get killed, because it shows," he proclaimed.

Another tactic that he employed to improve the show was to drop in on the "I Spy" and "Mission Impossible" sets to see how they paced themselves. He thought both were "well-done shows, but everyone with them has great enthusiasm, and that's what we've got to build up. We've got to fight to get it on the screen in spite of the schedule. When the script calls for action, we've got to have the real thing, rather than having the actors just talk it. This is high-style comedy-adventure and it isn't easy." If anyone associated with the series lacked enthusiasm for the project, R.J. more than made up for it with his own. Still, if he sensed someone was holding up the show without just cause, he would not hesitate to get that person canned.

The new R.J. was very upbeat on the set. He liked to keep everything moving, to get emotional and create confrontation. He looked the part too, wearing open-necked shirts and scads of gold chains. "I shake up everybody a bit on our set once in a while," he stated candidly, "but feel a better relationship results. I believe in conflict and discussion to get the best out of a situation where the schedule is the main concern." No one seemed to mind his disruptions. In fact, the producers were very happy with him and thought him rather cooperative. Said one staff member, "He's a really groovy-type guy, extremely considerate. He's a professional in the truest sense of the word—he's not tempermental or difficult. In fact, he bends over backward to be cooperative."

R.J.'s flare-ups, fairly well known among members of Hollywood, became less frequent as his career improved. At the height of the "It Takes a Thief" period he was asked about his temper and responded that now the "only thing that really bugs me is dishonesty." When asked if he liked TV, R.J. answered in a way that differed sharply from his response earlier in the decade. TV, he said, is "a challenge, it's a challenge to get and keep the audience interested. You've really got to be with it. When I was approached for the series I thought it would be a good vehicle for me. It was written with me in mind. I love the character. It's a hell of a lot of fun to play. All that larceny," he said with a wicked grin. "Isn't there a little larceny in all of us?"

By the time "It Takes a Thief" rolled into its second year, R.J. had already gained part ownership of the series, and was more involved than ever in its production. He'd also created a formula for success that kept the show fairly high in the ratings: "I like to have two or three good stars surrounding the thief. We show them first, then the thief's reaction to them. It's a simple format and it makes my character look good." De Sica would have been proud.

Although R.J. worked very hard, he had a good time. "It Takes a Thief" allowed him to incorporate many roles into the one of Alex Mundy, because the character often went under cover. This variety was just the sort of thing that made R.J. feel like he was truly acting rather than merely playing a two-dimensional image. "Bob really digs doing his role," said a show staff member. "It gives him depth because he's not always the same character. Actually, he's always Mundy but sometimes he parades as a writer, a photographer, or someone just for a cover."

Besides this formula there were some changes in the show's format. A new character was introduced, Alex Mundy's father, Alistair, who was played by Fred Astaire. If Alex had made the mistake of getting caught, his father, an even more formidable thief, had not. For this reason, Alex is the black sheep of the family, and the first meeting after many years between father and son almost ends bitterly. As luck would have it, however, Alex is forgiven his misdeed. He can count on his father's help in the SIA's next endeavor, which Alex is sure he can't carry out without the help of Dad, the only man who's better at the game than he is. Though the elder Mundy is retired, he decides that he can have a little fun helping out his son.

The idea worked well, and was also compatible with another innovation in the series: location shooting. By the second year, R.J. had convinced the studio that shooting in Europe would give the show a shot in the arm that would more than make up for the cost. That year five episodes were filmed on the continent. "It Takes a Thief" had achieved its flavor of international chic.

After its third season, however, the show was cancelled because its ratings, though respectable, did not show any sign of improving. R.J. didn't take it badly. "It Takes a Thief" had made him very much in demand. He also had a hunch the show would do well in syndication. His guess was correct, and the series later made him a tremendous amount of money, money he'd begin to put back into productions he'd been developing in his spare time. It was a way to become his own boss.

From "It Takes a Thief," which is still in syndication today, R.J. emerged a new man. He'd seen that he was a success, and that he could have the same success again if he wanted it. Coming to grips with his style of acting, he'd realized what was right for him. His unreasonable fantasy of having the whole world at his feet had been discarded for a whole new set of values. "I don't have any set goals," he said. "I just live my life. I just would like to be able to do as much as I can and hope my contributions will be felt and received well." He was more popular than ever.

If there were any doubts in Hollywood that he was in command of his life, then he dispelled them in 1971. Universal decided that it wanted him to play a detective in an upcoming TV movie, which the studio hoped would lead to a series. R.J. thought that his public image would be confused and ultimately tarnished by such a role. The personality he liked presenting to the public was of someone outside the law, working nonetheless for justice. He sought to evoke a sense of volunteerism in his audience. (He thought of it long before the current politicians did.) R.J. argued that a detective, who is paid for his work, can't advocate volunteerism without looking hypocritical. The case went to trial and the judge ruled in R.J.'s favor. The court also left open the option of a $5 million countersuit by R.J., but he never pursued it.

In the future, R.J. would play other TV roles similar to the one he played in "It Takes a Thief." He'd ultimately typecast himself. But it would be by his own choice. Never again would he be forced to play a part not to his liking.

While he became more visible at work, he became more private at home. Besides those times when the family came to the set, R.J. and Marion maintained a healthy distance between their home in Palm Springs and the bright lights of Hollywood. R.J. enjoyed being the family man and helping around the house. He cherished the simple things, for they helped keep his feet firmly planted on the ground. From the start of his career, he always believed that home should be a haven from the stress and strain of his professional life. Marion, the hub of this tranquil home life, had been R.J.'s best influence through these difficult years. She believed in him with a strength that forced him to bring out his best qualities. She helped him to believe in himself.

Ironically, his change for the better may have served to pull the rug out from under their marriage. Things were different now, and the situation that had brought and kept them together no longer existed. Not having built anything else between them, the marriage simply no longer existed.

In June 1970, they separated.

Robert Wagner in 1953 with his first convertible.
(*Courtesy of the* New York Post)

Robert in 1953, showing off at a friend's pool. *(Courtesy of the* New York Post)

(Below) Robert starred in *Prince Valiant* in 1954. Here he is seen with Victor McLaglen. *(Courtesy of 20th Century-Fox)*

He made *Beneath the 12-Mile Reef* in 1953, with Terry Moore. *(Courtesy of 20th Century-Fox)*

(Below) He acted with Terry Moore again in the 1956 movie, *Between Heaven and Hell.* *(Courtesy of 20th Century-Fox)*

On his way to St. Louis, Missouri, to promote *The True Story of Jessie James* in 1957. *(Courtesy of the* New York Post)

(Below) He spent a night on the town with The McGuire Sisters. From left: Christine, Phyllis, and Dorothy, 1957. *(Courtesy of the* New York Post)

(Right) Robert in a soulful mood from *All the Fine Young Cannibals,* 1961. *(Courtesy MGM)*

(Left) In 1962, Robert acted in *The War Lover.* *(Courtesy of Columbia Pictures)*

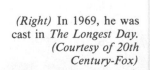

(Right) In 1969, he was cast in *The Longest Day.* *(Courtesy of 20th Century-Fox)*

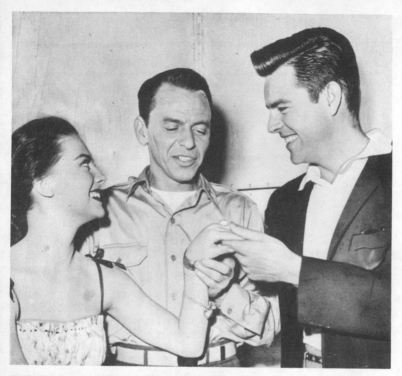

(Above) Robert showing off bride-to-be Natalie Wood's engagement ring to Frank Sinatra, 1957. *(Courtesy of the* New York Post)

(Left) The first honeymoon, 1958. *(Courtesy of Hollywood Press Syndicate)*

A wedding kiss in Scottsdale, Arizona, 1957.
(Courtesy of AP Photo)

Robert carrying his new bride off the train at Penn Station, 1958. *(Louis Liotta,* New York Post)

(Left) He and his second wife, Marion Marshall, pose on the courthouse steps in 1963. *(Courtesy of the New York Post)*

(Below) Natalie Wood and Warren Beatty in *Splendor in the Grass*, 1961. *(Courtesy of Warner Brothers)*

(Left) At home with Natalie and new baby, Courtney, 1974. *(Courtesy of the* New York Post)

Robert with Natalie in a scene from *Cat on a Hot Tin Roof*, 1976. *(Courtesy of NBC)*

(Left to right) Angie Dickinson, Dennis Weaver, R.J., and Lesley Ann Warren in "Pearl" miniseries, 1978. *(Courtesy of ABC)*

Robert with Freeway, the family dog on "Hart to Hart," 1979. *(Courtesy of ABC)*

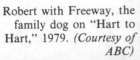

(Left to right) Kate, R.J., Natalie, Courtney, and Natasha. *(Courtesy of the* New York Post)

With "Heart to Heart" co-star Stefanie Powers on location in Vail, Colorado, 1980. *(Courtesy of ABC)*

The fifty-five foot yacht, Splendour, 1981. *(Courtesy of AP Photos)*

(Left) With daughter Courtney at his first public appearance since Natalie's death. He played in an American Heart Association benefit softball game, 1982. (Courtesy of AP Photos)

Robert with Jill St. John, 1985. (Courtesy of the New York Post)

Robert as Paul Newman's stiffest racing competitor in *Winning*, 1969.
(Courtesy of Universal Pictures)

Robert Wagner as Alexander Mundy in "It Takes a Thief," 1968.
(Courtesy of ABC)

=16=

Second Time Around

Since their divorce in 1962, Natalie and R.J. had rarely seen one another. Occasionally they'd talked over the phone. They had separate lives, and never again would they share them with each other. Or so they thought. But there was always something there, a feeling that never managed to die outright. Neither of them noticed it, really, and if they did, they never acknowledged it, at least not to the public. Somehow, though, their divorce was final only in the eyes of the law. As Natalie explained a few years after their second marriage, "We may have separated, but we never stopped loving each other. And gradually we realized we never were as happy with anyone else as we were with each other. Our life together never really ended; it was just interrupted." Their coming together the second time was more gradual than the first. But when the process started, they did not even know it had begun.

It was 1970 and "It Takes a Thief" was still doing very well in the ratings. R.J. was usually too tired after a long day on the set to socialize much in the evenings, but one night, he decided to accept an invitation to a dinner party. He'd go alone, without even a date. He was pensive these days, his pending divorce from Marion having made him think more deeply about the direction his life was taking. A girl on a date with him, or, for that matter, any companion that night, would have been bored out of her mind. R.J., ever the considerate gentleman, didn't like to disappoint a woman. But perhaps he had other reasons for going alone.

Natalie was at dinner. No surprise; the hosts, Linda and John Foreman, had called him up to make sure that this would not be indelicate of them. They called Natalie as well. Neither one was in the least put off by such a prospect. At the time, Natalie was still riding high from the success of *Bob & Carol & Ted & Alice.* At its completion, instead of taking a one-time fee of $750,000, she'd taken a percentage of the profits. Now she was well on her way to making $3 million from the controvertial smash-hit comedy about sexual mores. Success always sat well with Natalie, and she was radiant at dinner.

Had it been another time, R.J. might have retreated from the weight of her enormous achievement. Now he was his own man, with a winning TV series and legions of respectful fans. Of course, he was never the sort to lower himself to one-upmanship. There's no doubt, however, that a winning streak has a great deal to do with the kind of self-confidence you project. Both Natalie and R.J. were glowing with it, even if R.J. was in a reticent mood.

By the time everyone settled down to dinner, R.J. and Natalie were deep in conversation. "We talked all evening," Natalie recalled. "It was bittersweet. He walked me to the car. It was raining, and he was worried about my driving home to Bel Air by myself. He said, 'Are you happy?' What I didn't realize was that he was at the party alone because he and his wife had just separated."

In his mind, R.J. thought the question had been more philosophical than propositional, but to his emotions it had been the opposite. "The next day he sent me roses and a little note," Natalie recalled. "I sat and cried for a while, and thought that was that."

Emotions have this funny way of being misinterpreted, however, and R.J. was soon thinking about other women again. One of these women was Tina Sinatra, then twenty-two. R.J. had become good friends with the Sinatra clan and found Tina a delightful young lady, far more intelligent than her public persona suggested. They became involved, to the point where R.J. even went to live with Tina in her Century City apartment in Nevada, where they often flew kites on sunny afternoons, like two carefree kids living it up after the school bell dismissed them. They became engaged in late 1970, but the romance was over by 1971.

R.J.'s breakup with Tina had a lot to do with the continuing evolution of his independent bent. "I had a psychological breakout, like breaking out of jail," he said later, recalling the cathartic experience. "Before, I'd always wanted to satisfy others: there was a constant capitulation. That capitulation showed in my work. I projected a non-uniqueness."

In the meantime, R.J.'s divorce from Marion was made final. He appeared in October 1971 at the hearing before a superior court commissioner to obtain the uncontested decree that dissolved the eight-year marriage. Kate was seven at the time, and custody was awarded to Marion. As a settlement, R.J. would have to pay $1,250 per month in alimony plus 12.5 percent of his gross income above $150,000 yearly. He would also have to pay $400 monthly in child support.

R.J. was now a completely free man. Yet, he is not the type of person who relishes that kind of freedom. He needs to know that he's loved and cared for and that somebody will be there when he wants to talk honestly. At heart, he's a family man.

Natalie was not unaware of what had been happening in R.J.'s personal life. In fact, she'd been following it rather closely. The day the news came out that R.J. had broken up with Tina, Natalie went to lunch with a close girlfriend. "Bob's single again," Natalie told her friend. "Isn't that interesting?" R.J. was no less assiduous in following Natalie's romantic doings. Her marriage to agent-turned-producer Richard Gregson was on the rocks. All of Hollywood knew she had accused Gregson of infidelity and, after a big row in 1971, just two years after their marriage, she had thrown him out. R.J. hesitated at the impropriety of intruding but finally called Natalie. No specific plans were made during their conversation, but the ease with which they spoke made them each feel whole again. "When R.J. heard I was getting a divorce," Natalie recalled, "he phoned me. We had a lot of telephonic contact. Then

I just got on a plane [in the fall of 1971] and flew to Palm Springs, to the very house we lived in after we got married."

They did not rush down to City Hall to retie the knot. No romantic mad dash to that little office that churns out so many married couples. The first time around they had lived together a year before marrying; this time it would take them half as long to be sure. The second time, though, they waited to tell people that they were together, were, indeed, living together. They lived so quietly in Palm Springs that not even their best friends guessed. Natalie explained, a little over a year after they were remarried, "We were going together a very long time before anybody knew about it. First in Palm Springs and then in Lake Tahoe. Mickey Ziffren [novelist, good friend, and wife of her lawyer, Paul] gave me a birthday party last year. And halfway through the evening [the playwright] Leonard Gershe leaned over and said, 'Oh, I get it! You're together again!' "

Even after the marriage ceremony took place, this pleasant surprise registered on many faces. "People come up to us all the time," said a very happy R.J. in 1973. "They say, 'Oh, you're together! How nice.' "

In R.J.'s mind, there was a certain inevitability to the rematch. "We were both divorced," he recalled, "and we said, 'What the hell, we did have some good things together when we were too young to recognize them.' So we dated, secretly, for months. Everyone thinks we just casually met on the *Queen Elizabeth 2* — because the ship's captain spotted us together and tipped off the press. But by then we had been thinking of remarriage for a long time."

The transatlantic voyage must have encouraged the decision, no doubt. "It was the worst weather I have ever experienced," said Captain Mortimer Hemir. "Nobody in the ship had ever known winds of that velocity to last so long." During the freak Atlantic storm, Natalie and R.J. were forced to spend a lot of time alone in their cabin. They didn't mind a bit. When they docked in New

York, they admitted to "being in love again," Natalie said. "We plan to get married again too."

A few months before the wedding, they decided to go public and picked the most press-laden event of show business to appear together. When they arrived at the Oscars with their arms around each other, it was as if they were already remarried in the eyes of an astounded public.

The actual ceremony took place on July 16, 1972, aboard a yacht in Paradise Cove near Malibu. It was a small affair, with only family and close friends present. Natalie wore a long Mexican cotton dress. R.J. was in an open-necked shirt. There was a sense of gaiety, a joking atmosphere. Napkins and matchbooks were inscribed: "It's better the second time around." He was forty-two; she, thirty-three. After the guests left, they cruised around Catalina for nearly a week.

Gone was the starry-eyed, naïve young couple of the first marriage. After that breakup, R.J. hadn't been able to stand reminders of Natalie around the house. He gave their set of barstools to his sister, Mary. When they got back together, she returned them. They were a little scarred, but were still comfortable. Their second marriage was a lot like that. The second time around, they were grown-ups, each responsible for a daughter, both hoping the whole lot of them would form a family.

Natalie's pyschiatrist had finally convinced her not to hold grudges, and she brought to their remarriage a new candor. "We're both much more open with one another," she said. "If we have any negative thoughts, we don't harbor them, we talk about them. Before, if he hurt my feelings, I would just be silent about it and get in a bad mood and say, 'Oh, it's nothing, oh nothing,' when he asked me what was wrong. But now I can tell him what's wrong, so it can be dealt with."

One point of agreement was children. They both desperately wanted a child together. In July 1973, Natalie discovered she was pregnant. To pass the time until the baby's birth, she and R.J.

co-starred in a TV movie, "The Affair." Still waiting, the Wagner clan went to London for R.J.'s starring role in the BBC TV series "Colditz." They used the trip as the second marriage's second honeymoon, and brought Natasha and Kate with them. Tony Curtis kindly lent them his Chester Square residence, and they turned it into a temporary home. The girls loved watching the changing of the guard at Buckingham Palace and visiting the scary Tower. Several days, they visited their daddy on the set.

R.J. was delighted by his role in "Colditz" and welcomed the visits from his family. He was secure in the knowledge that he was doing a good job. "Not only do we have good scripts and marvelous actors," he enthused, "but the way we do this demands a level of acting I've never had to deliver before. We rehearse each show for ten days and then we try to tape it in one, though we often slop over to two and three taping days. But almost right off, you're on your feet and in there acting. It's genuinely communicative acting, one-on-one acting. You can't slough it, you've got to play it."

In the series about Allied prisoners at the formidable Nazi prison of Colditz Castle in Saxony, R.J. played an American pilot flying for the RAF. Captain Pat Reid, author of the books upon which the series was based, was a consultant on the show, and he fascinated R.J. with historical tales about the war camp. According to Reid, Colditz Castle was built by King Augustus the Strong of Poland over a medieval fortress on a promontory 250 feet above the River Mulde. The Germans kept a garrison there, one that was larger in number than the prisoners within! The castle itself was surrounded by enormous amounts of barbed wire. Even if escape was remotely feasible against these odds, the nearest friendly border was still over 400 miles away. R.J.'s eyes widened at the chance for derring-do, but he realized there was more to the story than mere adventure. "If you think this is a prisoner-of-war story in terms of *The Great Escape,*" he explained, "you couldn't be more wrong. It's not so much a story of war and prison as of people, of humanity. It's as if Colditz is a microcosm of existence in which these men are accidentally thrust together—Poles and

French as well as British. Escaping from an escape-proof prison is the prime motivation—it's the motivating force of their lives."

After a very long labor, Courtney Brooke, their good-luck symbol, their sign of renewed love, was born on March 9, 1974. It wasn't easy. "I had no problem with Natasha," Natalie recalled, "but with Courtney, it was a disaster. I was fully awake and watched the whole thing in a mirror until they ran into difficulties and had to perform an emergency cesarean. The umbilical cords was wrapped around her neck three times and a whole team of doctors were running around in white coats, yelling, 'Emergency section—emergency pediatric intensive care—get up here on the double!' The last thing I remember them doing is throwing a white sheet over the mirror so I couldn't see the knife. I kept yelling, 'Cut, I want a retake!' I felt like I was on the wrong set and the scene was from somebody else's picture."

When the seven-pound, five-ounce baby was presented to R.J., he felt like he'd won an Academy Award. But now that their family was complete, the media began to look at them once again as "hot copy."

Their marriage the second time around certainly didn't have the earth-shattering cataclysmic effect the first had had on the entertainment world, but it came close. In many respects, the second time around, with all the complexities inherent in being married to the same person twice, provided an even greater field day for the press. Editors loved it for all the space they could fill explaining the nuances of the couple's romantic history. Only the Burton-Taylor liaison could offer more.

The interviews would unfold this way: They would be asked how long they had been married. They would respond, "Which time?" Then Natalie would good-naturedly break it down for the snickering reporter. "We've been married eight years, but that's over nine years, or nine and a half. You see, we lived together for one year before we got married the first time and for six months before we got married the second time. Do you have that?"

And then there were the kids. "As for our children," R.J. would say with a grin, "we have his, hers, and ours. Kate, who is mine, Natasha, who is Nat's, and Courtney, who is ours."

In addition to the confusion created by their wide-ranging brood, R.J. and Natalie would celebrate all their anniversaries, twice as many as most couples, as well as the anniversaries of when they met and remet. They each had kept their wedding rings from their first marriage and now wore them on chains around their necks. They were faithful to the rituals of family, with an eye toward making this second marriage last.

Toward this end they implemented some of the rules they'd tried to stick to the first time. The most important of these, now doubly so because of the presence of children in their lives, was never to work on the same project together, and never to work simultaneously. Asked about the chances of their working together, R.J. would usually respond that "we're not especially interested in working as a team." To which Natalie would add, "We want to be a team in real life—and we are."

If the questions continued, R.J. might sometimes let a little irritation show through his carefully maintained facade. Once, rather heatedly, he told a reporter, "Both of us couldn't work on a series at the same time. We'd never have any home life. Someone has to be home. If she worked on my series, she'd have to get up at six every morning and wouldn't be finished until nine at night. There wouldn't be anyone home with the kids for seven or eight months. A series is very demanding, the most demanding work any actor can undertake. It's especially hard on a woman. We have two small daughters [Kate was then living with her mother], and we made an agreement that one or the other of us must be home at all times—unless we can take them with us. I know from experience [his long years of military boarding schools] how important it is for kids to be with parents."

Together the family would ski, play tennis, swim. R.J. had always used sports as a way to relax, and now with the children, they became even more fun. His frolics with them encouraged him to again be active on a regular basis. Sports allowed R.J. to channel his pent-up frustrations into an area where it was safe to be aggressive. Being a very gifted athlete allowed him the luxury of being superior to most of his competitors. From the time he won the celebrity golf open back in the late 1950s by beating Sam Snead, R.J. had always been Hollywood's top athlete. Paul Newman called him "the greatest natural athlete I've ever known. It's really quite incredible."

Besides golf, tennis, Ping-Pong, motorcycling, squash, and waterskiing, R.J. enjoys fishing. "I have a water orientation," he says. "Long ago I was offered a swimming and diving scholarship to USC, but I chose Twentieth Century–Fox university instead. There was also the great shooting craze as well," he said. "Bob Stack put a gun in my hand for target practice and I loved it. Eventually it wore off. Like all actors, I get involved. I find something new, become passionately involved, and then drop it. You might say that most actors are basically fickle, or that they tend to run around mastering one situation after another."

The one situation that he consistently tried to make better was his family life. Domestic tranquility has always been the boost he needs to feel confident in his acting. In fact, the two elements go hand in hand. Hadn't he lost Natalie the first time because of his faltering career? And didn't his career help him get back together with her? With their second marriage, everything was in balance. "I've always believed that it's very important with regard to the quality of your performance to have an outside life, a life totally divorced from the cameras," he said. "Because if you can let that life filter through you in a positive way, that's when you're really able to bring something to a part and make your character come to life. It's been happening for me since we got back together. The last several years have been the happiest in my life," he said in 1979.

So it would be. But only a year after they were married, stories were already circulating that their marriage was on the rocks. The Wagners did all they could to put a stop to the rumors. Friends who observed their steady and loving relationship scoffed at the gossip. Instead, they spoke of the ten-year aging process for fine wines. Nobody missed the analogy. R.J. and Natalie had matured a great deal since their divorce, and they would talk about what a help this was to their second time around. "I find it easier to be married now," R.J. said. "Because a lot of time has gone by. And a lot of experiences." The Wagners, now in their prime, were once again the perfect couple.

Of their first attempt at perfection, Natalie said, "I was very young and naïve in many ways. I thought marriage would be like some magic potion that would make everything right. It wasn't," she said. "When you get a little older and get to know yourself a little better, you develop a tremendous sense of appreciation for certain people. My separation from R.J. made me appreciate him more as a person. You don't realize how much you love or need someone until he's not there anymore. When you're young, it's easy to take things for granted."

17

R. J.'s Angels

For all their hard work as actors, the Wagners made more money behind the screen than on it. After their second marriage, they formed a second production company, RONA II, for "Robert and Natalie the second time around." It was soon after Courtney's birth, and they were anxious to get some behind-the-scenes action in TV and films. Production was ideal. They'd be involved in their profession, but not to the exclusion of their family.

Two veteran producers got to them first. They convinced the couple who said they would never again act together to co-star in a TV movie. At the same time, the producers, Aaron Spelling and Leonard Goldberg, unwittingly gave R.J. and Natalie their first big production lesson.

"It began in 1973," Goldberg explained to *TV Guide*. "We had a good TV-movie script called 'The Affair,' about a crippled woman falling in love with a handsome man who is unaware, at first, that she is handicapped. It was a natural teaming for Natalie and R.J.," said Goldberg, who, along with Spelling, had teamed up with Lord Lew Grade and Barry Diller to get "The Affair" off the ground. Their big concern was how to get R.J. and Natalie. "She wasn't doing TV at the time," he said, "and he was signed for big movies like *The Towering Inferno* and *Midway*. He had one hit TV series, 'It Takes a Thief,' which was already doing fantastically well in syndication, and he didn't seem inclined to go back into television.

"But we were able to get the Wagners to read the script. They liked it. However, we felt it was necessary to sweeten the pot for them in order to nail down the deal. They accepted the pot-sweetener. On page six of the hundred-and-eighty-page contract there was a provision that within one year they could develop a series pilot, in which neither had to play a role. It was a nice gesture but there wasn't much risk in it for us or for ABC. If nothing was submitted by the Wagners during the year, the network would simply have to pay an additional twenty-five thousand dollars."

R.J. and Natalie had read the script in their Beverly Hills living room, surrounded by the children they always vowed to be with. They were diligent in their quest to be a family first, but this diligence gave them more time to mull over scripts. And they really liked "The Affair." "It's a wonderful role for Natalie," R.J. said. For Natalie to be doing a TV movie, however, meant that she felt her career needed a boost. Never mind that the page six provision would someday be seen as a coup seldom if ever achieved in Hollywood. This would not be the last time that Natalie would seek refuge in the lower echelon of Hollywood's hierarchy, the place where R.J. was one of the lords and fast becoming an internationally acclaimed superstar.

It was not long before the page six provision from the contract for "The Affair" reared its head again in the Spelling/Goldberg office. Goldberg's accountants asked him if they just should have ABC send over the $25,000 to the Wagners. "No," Goldberg said. "We want to maintain the goodwill of the Wagners because we may need them again some day. I think we'd better go through the motions of getting some sort of series idea over to the network."

He recalled that he "had come up with a terrible concept called "The Alley Cats." "My partner, Aaron Spelling, looked at it and said, 'You ought to be ashamed of yourself.' R.J. looked at it and said, 'That's possibly the worst idea I've ever seen in my life.' He and Natalie figured, however, that they had nothing to lose.

They'd get more than the $25,000 if a miracle happened and we wangled a small development deal out of the network. We figured we had nothing to lose because the idea probably could never work, but in the meantime we were making the Wagners happy. So we put some writers on the project, changed the name to 'Charlie's Angels,' and eventually sent it over to Fred Silverman after he had moved over to ABC from CBS."

Not a single person involved ever thought anything would come of it, but the success of "Charlie's Angels" needs no elaboration. Freddie Silverman loved the idea, and so did the American public. The Wagners' company, RONA II, was entitled to approximately 50 percent of the show's earnings, despite the fact that R.J. and Natalie had had nothing to do with any part of its production.

After this enormous success, R.J. began to chastise himself for not getting into independent production sooner. He rushed into producing and co-starring in "Madame Sin" with Bette Davis, a TV movie in which she played a power-crazed female Machiavelli who gains control of some Polaris submarines. R.J. was hoping the two-hour movie could be the basis for a series. He was thinking big. "I was really disappointed that it didn't sell on a weekly basis," he said, "but some Orientals protested they had been depicted in an evil way." R.J. was dismayed, but the continuing success of "Charlie's Angels" lessened the blow.

While on a family vacation in the south of France, the Wagners received word that Spelling and Goldberg had allegedly defrauded them out of half a million dollars. "It comes as a complete surprise to us," R.J. said when he first heard the news, adding good-naturedly, "We could use the half-million bucks to pay for this vacation."

The alleged fraud had to do with a transfer of money from the "Charlie's Angels" account to another Spelling/Goldberg production, "Starsky and Hutch." While "Charlie's Angels" was doing fabulously well, "Starsky and Hutch" was foundering and would soon be cancelled. Jennifer Martin, an attorney in the ABC contracts department, thought she had discovered some nefarious activities when she noticed the money being diverted from "Charlie's Angels," first to the "Starsky and Hutch" series, then straight to Spelling and Goldberg for supposed exclusivity fees. She realized the production duo had been working exclusively for ABC for several years and had never before received such a fee.

When Martin queried her superiors, she was rebuffed and told to mind her own business. One executive, Ronald Sunderland, yelled at her. "Okay. You want to know what it's really for?" he asked. "They're [Spelling and Goldberg] fucking the Robert Wagners out of their money. We've been putting it into 'Starsky and Hutch' up until now, but since 'Starsky' is off the air, the money's got to go somewhere else, so we're calling it exclusivity." Later Sunderland said his remarks were uttered in anger and taken out of context.

Martin would not be stopped. She sent memos all the way to the top, and ABC finally launched an internal investigation. It found nothing wrong, except for Martin's work. She was fired. In retrospect, it seems ABC miscalculated that move, since it sent Martin scurrying to the press. With no reasonable explanation and no cooperation from inside her company, she felt she had no other choice. The aftermath of her actions resulted in a year of investigation, which eventually led the Los Angeles D.A. to state he believed no improprieties had been committed and that the case should not be brought to trial.

What had really happened is an object lesson in the inner workings of a TV series. When a network contracts for a show, it only foots part of the bill. With "Charlie's Angels," for example, each segment cost $623,000. ABC would only pay $583,000. This left a deficit of $800,000 to $900,000 every season. Only when a show goes into syndication is this deficit erased. It is then that the profits start to roll in. Producers are left in the middle fretting and worrying about cost overruns until syndication brings on the good times.

Spelling and Goldberg, two of Hollywood's best worriers, had finally had enough of "Starsky and Hutch." They'd been begging for months for more money from the network. After advancing some cash, ABC would give no more. "I can't help you," ABC vice president George Reeves told them. "Don't even come ask me, because everybody here has had it up to their ears with 'Starsky and Hutch.' " There was, however, some extra cash that was supposed to go to "Charlie's Angels," and it was suggested by William Hayes, Spelling/Goldberg's attorney, that some of that cash go to the troubled series. The network agreed. "If you want to allocate it that way, it's up to you," Reeves said. "Just write me a letter and tell me what you're going to do so we can put it on our records."

The money was eventually supposed to be returned to "Angels" and that's apparently what was going on when the money was switched to the "exclusivity" heading. The D.A. saw it that way anyway, and the Wagners were satisfied. For the record, R.J. and Natalie said they felt very confident that Spelling/Goldberg had done nothing wrong. "Angelgate," as it was dubbed, was over.

But not for R.J. He learned more about producing from that one incident than he would have if he'd apprenticed for years at one of the networks. The most important lesson he came away with was that producing meant high stakes. It also dangled enormous purses. R.J. felt ready to gamble.

18

"Switch"

In the mid-1970s, as Natalie's star began to dim somewhat, R.J.'s was on the rise. He signed for his second TV series, "Switch," co-starring with Eddie Albert. The adventure show, which ran for two years, and is still in syndication, paired two characters who were on opposite sides of the law, one a rogue thief, the other a policeman. The thief has been reformed and the cop has retired from the force. Together they team up to solve extraordinary crimes, and solve crimes in an extraordinary way.

Thankfully for R.J., the relationship between the two characters took precedence over the hackneyed story lines. "What else is there," remarked Albert halfway through the show's run. "It can't be the plots. They're the same as for every other detective show on the air." Predictably, R.J. played Pete Ryan, the rogue thief. For once, he didn't worry about being typecast. "Pete is an ex-con man, a man who lives against the law," Eddie Albert said about his screen partner. "He knows a fellow who can get into the safe at midnight. Mac [his own character, ex-flatfoot Frank MacBride] doesn't want to know about that, but Pete gets the information and he's in no position to complain." MacBride, of course, likes things done by the book, and the two of them are as often as not fighting over the procedure they should use.

As usual, R.J. was very attentive to his audience. He welcomed the tour buses that came to the set and talked to the stunned tourists, folks from the heartland who never expected such a cordial welcome. He even consented to go on a national tour in

1976 on behalf of "Switch." Natalie, who had little to do on her own, went with him. "Working in episodic TV, you seldom get out," he said. "This tour with Natalie has been wonderful, being able to get a real response from people who watch you."

Meeting and greeting his fans in this way was further testimony to his old-fashioned professionalism. It's the gesture of a true working actor. In his early days in Hollywood, when he learned to survive on his workaholic nature and his ability to charm Louella and Hedda, he also learned to use that extra drive at all times. Other actors with more secure beginnings never feel that need to cover all the bases. Natalie was one of this rank. When their careers start ebbing, they don't have the experience to get up and fight for the public. Early on, that drive saved R.J.; now it was taking him to the top.

He won the lead role in *Airport '79 Concorde,* with Susan Blakely. A few months after its completion, he admitted he hadn't seen it yet. "But at least the critics didn't get me," he said. "I came out unscathed. If you can walk away from something like that without getting your head blown off, you should consider yourself fortunate."

A year earlier, he had tackled the lead role in "Pearl," a miniseries about the events surrounding the bombing of Pearl Harbor. The whole family went with him to Hawaii for the filming, making a splendid vacation of the whole thing. Sort of. There were rumors that Natalie insisted on going to keep an eye on R.J. Angie Dickinson, his co-star, had recently separated from her husband, Burt Bacharach. The Wagner family, extended now by tutors and pets, ignored the idle chat, however, and had a marvelous time relaxing on the beach. Soon after, Natalie tried to convince R.J. to request a few weeks off to accompany her to the Cannes Film Festival, where she was to promote her latest movie, a critical and box-office failure called *Meteor.* Although the memory of her time there with Warren Beatty haunted R.J., he agreed to go. Then a family emergency intervened. Seven-year-old Natasha was stricken with a double hernia, and all plans had to be cancelled.

The pressures of being a full-time mother were taking their toll. Natalie, devoted to her kids, felt they were now old enough for her to resume her career for short stretches. "If a great part for Natalie would materialize," R.J. said, "I'd gladly stay home and take care of the kids. She looks after them while I'm working and is a terrific mother, but I wouldn't hesitate to take her place if a wonderful role came along for her."

The trouble was, there were few roles at all that were coming her way. It was a particularly poignant time, because Natalie was just beginning to feel she had something to offer acting. "I went through a period when I was fed up with work," she explained. "It started with the feeling that I had nothing to offer as a person outside the parts that I played, because I hadn't had any living experience beyond that. I wanted to define myself in terms of what I am instead of what I do. Now, though, I'm beginning to feel again that acting is part of my life and that I have something to give to it."

There was little to give it to. Natalie was getting older and the parts weren't coming. Times were rough for her, and they would not get any easier. Nature was taking its toll, and Natalie, though still very beautiful, was beginning to show signs of age. She was not prepared for the transition. She wanted nothing of that demotion that is the curse of aging Hollywood stars. She refused to do screen tests. This probably cost her several roles, including Daisy in *The Great Gatsby.*

In the same period, she made another flop, *The Last Married Couple in America.* According to her sister, Lana, Natalie was beginning to get frantic. No longer was she the cool operator who could begin a stringent diet before a movie started production. No longer could she diet so well that she would look smashing for the camera. She needed diet pills, and these caused mood swings and stretches of prolonged irritability. When her agent sent her a script called *The Mirror Crack'd,* she finished reading it and became furious. It was about an aging actress who refused to give up her vanity. Natalie threw down the script and started cursing. It was too close to home.

Fortunately, another part came her way, but it was in the minor realm of TV. And to add insult to injury, in Natalie's view, it was a remake. But she bit her lip and took the part in "From Here to Eternity," the role Deborah Kerr had made famous. A year later, Natalie decided to actively pursue a career on the stage. She began working with Arvin Brown, the director who had successfully staged Broadway's *A View From the Bridge,* on a play about the Russian princess Anastasia. She also signed for what she deemed a little trifle: an off-beat sci-fi movie called *Brainstorm,* about an estranged couple reunited by a machine. It would co-star a bright young Oscar-winning actor, Christopher Walken.

But all that was in the future, and R.J. realized Natalie needed a morale boost right away. Years ago, Spencer Tracy had introduced him to Laurence Olivier. Over the years, they'd kept up a casual friendship. Then, as R.J. recalled, "this part just dropped out of the sky." Olivier was getting together a cast for a Granada Television/NBC co-production of Tennessee Williams' *Cat on a Hot Tin Roof.* Olivier, one of the greatest actors of the twentieth century, would play Big Daddy, and he wanted R.J. for the role of his son Brick. Natalie was chosen to play the flirtatious Maggie. The Wagners were both enthralled.

"You never know when you're going to be hot or cold," said R.J. "I've been doing it for twenty-five years, and I'm still working, so I consider myself a success. But I've taken a lot of body blows. In order to keep working, I've had to do the TV series. But they're nothing to be snobbish about. They're damned hard to do. I work ten hours a day, nine months a year, so I can afford to do something meaningful like *Cat on a Hot Tin Roof.*"

"It was a lucky break for us," Natalie admitted. "We rehearsed for four weeks in London, blocked it just like a play. The whole thing was taped in nine days."

Olivier rebuilt the dressing rooms so that the Wagners could watch each other onstage and baby-sit at the same time. "Working together is easier if you're married," R.J. said. "You can cue each other in bed, in the shower, over the breakfast table. What's hard is turning it off after a dramatic scene so you don't take Maggie and Brick home at night. Still, it was probably the best working experience we've ever had," he said.

As if a good omen, the show was scheduled to air on December 6, 1978. "We won't forget the date," Natalie said. "That's our anniversary. Well, not really. It's the date of our first important date." On that evening twenty-two years before, R.J. and Natalie had first made love.

=19=

"Hart to Hart"

R.J. was the hottest he'd ever been, and just around the corner lay more great opportunities. And again, it was Leonard Goldberg who was laying the golden eggs. In 1970, "I Dream of Jeannie" writer Sidney Sheldon (who has since made millions peddling glitz to Hollywood), came up with a series idea called "Double Twist." Goldberg shoved it away in his drawer. Eight years later, when the public seemed to be craving a light, urbane adventure series, he resurrected the idea. Anyway, he thought, it seemed at least as lousy as "Alley Cats," which later aired as "Charlie's Angels," the success story of the decade. Why not pursue it? Screenwriter/director Tom Mankiewicz, son of the Hollywood mogul Joseph L. Mankiewicz, began reworking it.

"When Tom was finished," Goldberg recalled, "I realized that we were in a box. There is only one current actor capable of playing that suave, lifted-eyebrow sort of action humor—and his name is Robert Wagner. If I couldn't have him, I'd have to scrap the entire project."

Once again, R.J. was very, very hot. "He was doing 'Pearl,' he'd done 'Switch,' he'd done 'Cat on a Hot Tin Roof' with Laurence Olivier, he had the top role in the big movie *Airport '79 Concorde.* "

Goldberg didn't hesitate one minute in trying to get R.J. to do the series for him: "I sent Tom Mankiewicz to see R.J. in Hawaii, where he was on location for 'Pearl.' R.J. liked the pilot script and made several valuable suggestions for updating it. Then, when he returned to Los Angeles, we sat down to talk business. First of all, he said that Stefanie Powers had worked well with him in 'It Takes a Thief,' and that he wanted her to play opposite him if he should agree to do the series. Secondly, we had to come up with another 'page six provision' in the contract, only this time it would be two additional development projects for Natalie and R.J.'s production company, Rona II. I gulped but said okay. And that's how we and ABC acquired R.J. as a partner again and got him to play Jonathan Hart in 'Hart to Hart.' " R.J. got 50 percent of the "Hart to Hart" series for RONA II as well, and eventually became the show's executive producer.

In this series R.J. played a self-made millionaire whose wife, Jennifer, played by Stefanie Powers, is a journalist. Since they are rich and insatiably curious and love to travel, they can "matriculate in and out of some rather stylish surroundings. In addition," R.J. continued, "because they are people of some wealth and celebration, they find themselves in exciting circumstances with exciting people. Their journalistic attitude makes them seek out the whys and wherefores of every situation. And what's most wonderful is that story ideas for this kind of set-up are plentiful." Every week the Harts found themselves in the midst of some high-class dirty dealings in which their friends would need help. The Harts would find out who the culprits were and solve the crime.

It was a partnership show, and the choice of his wife was crucial to its success. "I never thought of anyone else to play my wife other than Stefanie Powers," R.J. proclaimed. "We worked previously on an episode of 'It Takes a Thief,' and I liked her a lot. Her style of acting is perfect for me. She's a terrific contributor and a total professional. I'm thoroughly comfortable doing the show with her." She was his perfect complement in their dangerous escapades because from her confident bearing "you had the sense that she could get out of anything," R.J. explained. "If she had to run through reeds or swim up a river, she'd be there." As the lovable valet/chauffeur, who watched the Harts' antics with a raised eyebrow, the production company chose character actor

Lionel Stander. R.J., who had the right to approve casting, whole-heartedly backed that decision.

The series had other less typical attributes to recommend it. "We create the sort of couple people would like to be," Powers explained. "They are two people having a love affair who happen to be married."

" 'Dallas,' 'Dynasty,' 'Falcon Crest,' they all depict the wealthy as nasty, conniving, trying to mess each other over," added script-writer Mankiewicz. " 'Hart' is a warm fantasy of wealth. I think Americans right now aspire to wealth, and deep down, want to believe you can be rich *and* decent. The Harts address that wish."

For R.J., it was the kind of show he could play in his sleep. He was the same old charmer, irresistible to the women and a paragon of sophistication and attentiveness from tip to stern. It never seemed to bother him that for his entire successful TV career, he has essentially typecast himself. Of course, there is an enormous difference between chosing one's roles and being forced to play them. And there is a difference as well between being a pretty boy and being the supercool man about town who's capable of solving complex crimes.

That cool sometimes came to a boil, however, when certain assertions were made regarding precedents for the show's format. R.J. never acknowledged that "Hart to Hart" had been conceived with *The Thin Man* in mind. When once asked about the undenia-ble similarities between the two, he became positively hostile. "Actually, 'Hart to Hart' is a high-style comedy-love story," he said, "involving two people who get caught up in adventure week after week. We never thought of the 'Thin Man' series when we took on this show. Naturally, I'd be happy if we could provide the same joy that William Powell and Myrna Loy did in their series." (Powell and Loy, of course, did the movies. The series starred Peter Lawford and Phyllis Kirk.)

Neither would R.J. tolerate the series ever being labeled a detec-tive show. Since he never wanted to play a detective and had already sued Universal over the matter, it's understandable why he would bristle at anyone with the temerity to suggest such a notion. "Of course, I'm not a private investigator on this series," he'd respond. "You need a license to be one. I've never played a cop on any of my series. In fact, I won a suit against Universal seven years ago when they tried to force me into playing a detective. The Harts deal with crime from outside the law. That's another thing. We're not always involved with crime. There will be plenty of shows where only human relations will be explored." Of course, much to his dismay, this never turned out to be true.

The heated exchanges he had on these topics were some of the few times R.J. let his composure crack. Even though he had learned to master a calm exterior, R.J. continued to be an emotional and tempermental man. To his credit, this demeanor has sometimes helped him be a more constructive collaborative force. He is the kind of guy who doesn't easily forget. On the plus side, his loyalty sometimes overwhelms. He recommended Natalie's former secretary, *Boys in the Band* playwright Mart Crowley, to executives on "Hart to Hart." The result? Crowley was named a producer of the show.

When the "Hart to Hart" pilot aired in the fall of 1979, it was a big success, and everyone felt confident that the series would have a long run. They were right. The show ran for five seasons, but was unexpectedly cancelled in 1984 due to behind-the-scenes problems. Among them: R.J.'s dissatisfaction with the writers, all of whom he fired.

When the news of the show's cancellation reached the public, "Hart to Hart"'s loyal audience responded by laying siege to the network's offices with an avalanche of mail protesting the decision. The letters didn't change anything, but they did prove R.J. was more popular than ever.

20
Happy Days

The Wagners' home life was as normal as the two stars could make it. And they tried very hard to make it so. This drive to be ordinary was eased by the fact that they liked doing things together and with their children. They were both very attentive to the kids and tried to give them stability in an environment well known for its shaky foundations. When R.J. traveled on location, he would often bring the family with him. He would also take time out from shooting a series to spend a little time at home. When it came to fatherhood, he was in his element. This was what he had meant to be in life: a suave bon vivant who's also a breadwinner with a wholesome all-American family to come home to. He played the part with more sincerity than he ever brought to bear on any of his performances.

Of course, Natalie had millions of dollars of her own. But this didn't change the schematics of the Wagner household. From the time of their first marriage, it was obvious that Natalie enjoyed playing the dependent housewife who waited patiently at home for her man to bring home the bacon and light up her life; of course, very few other American women lived that way. When the real world somehow made its way past the front door, though, it always found Natalie barricaded behind her star status, which in turn, was hidden by her mock apron. Nevertheless, harmony reigned in the Wagner household, and despite the fact that Natalie found the kitchen as mysterious as the other side of the moon, she was as good a mother as R.J. was a father.

Furthermore, Natalie always looked at motherhood as something more sought after than forced upon her. "There's nothing more fascinating than watching kids grow," she once said as she began trying to get her career back on track. And she meant it. Whenever she could, however, she would dabble in her career. In that sense alone she was a modern woman. "For women," she explained in 1979, "a career and a family have often been an either/or proposition. Either you had a career or you got married and had kids. And it was always very difficult to blend the two. Whether it was true or not, that's the way it was always presented. But now, with the changing role of women, I think people are beginning to realize you can be a good wife and mother and pursue a career at the same time. I'm glad the rigidity of that kind of old-fashioned thinking is changing. My mother was a wonderful mother and woman. But she literally thinks of her motherhood as sacrificing her life for the sake of her children. I think if she had been able to express herself in some way in addition to raising a family, she would have been much happier." Obviously, Natalie was thinking that perhaps her mother would have been less rigid in pushing her relentlessly toward success if she herself had had something else going on.

The Wagners were forever serious when it came to maintaining that balance between careers and family life. Explaining her ideas on how best to maintain a marriage, Natalie said: "It's really a question of trying out how to use your time the best way and be flexible. I think the main thing is to try and be together as much as possible, so that you are with your kids enough and with your husband enough and doing your own thing. We have been asked to do a series together but can you imagine? We would never be at home with the children. It was out of the question."

Natalie's domesticity by choice during the early 1970s finally came into its own when she had Courtney. "I was so happy, and full of emotion. Breast-feeding my baby was the most fulfilling experience of my life. I think good mother's milk is really the best food for a new baby. Being able to give to my daughter in this special way is truly beautiful and right." She'd often feed her daughter in the living room, surrounded by the rest of her family.

By the time Natalie thought seriously about returning to work, "most producers," she recalled, "assumed I had retired for good." But with R.J.'s blessing, she would never put her career before her duty as a mother. "If I had another child now I think I'd take another couple of years off, because when they're very young I'm not able to be away from them," she said. When she did start acting again, and was finding it difficult to regain the lost ground, R.J. was gallantly supportive. Upon completing a picture, R.J. would give Natalie a gold coin inscribed with the name of her movie and the name of her character. When R.J. was working and she had free time, Natalie would run around the house frantically, making sure everything was in order for her husband's return. They tried very hard to please each other.

Shortly after they were remarried, they bought a sixty-foot yacht. "After my family and my work, my greatest obsession is the sea," R.J. once said. But of course, they both always loved the sea and loved to get away from the prying eyes of the world, just as they had during their first marriage. They named the new yacht *Splendour,* after one of Natalie's most successful movies. (For R.J.'s sake the *u* was added to differentiate between the happiness of the present and the unhappiness he suffered while *Splendor in the Grass* was filming and Natalie was falling in love with Warren Beatty.) R.J. good-naturedly named the yacht's dinghy *The Prince Valiant,* after the movie in which he gave what he thought was his worst performance ever.

It was a comfortable life. At their parties, liquor flowed and the guests always seemed to stay later than they'd planned. R.J. would get into long political discussions, talking about the dangers of ocean pollution. Natalie would flutter about checking on each guest. They included the rich, the famous, and the ordinary. Laurence Olivier, Elia Kazan, and David Niven often mingled with the Goldbergs, Spellings, other producers, and the locals. "These two must have more real chums than anyone in this town. I suppose it's because they're so real," David Niven said while observing a table in the Wagners' living room with a slew of silver-framed photographs of friends on it. Olivier, a good friend since the making of 'Cat on a Hot Tin Roof,' said of the Wagners, "The most dear couple. They really care."

They could still have fun, sometimes at the expense of others. At a party at Alan Ladd Jr.'s, R.J. and actor George Segal began roasting another guest, check-forger David Begelman. Other guests said the jibes got out of hand and some deemed the razzing "tasteless, vulgar, and stinging." They kept quiet after producer Ray Stark yelled, "It's not funny any longer, boys."

For the most part though, R.J. did most of his socializing at home during this period. A usual evening was dinner with his family and maybe a movie. He didn't need the high life to make him content. He had a wife whom he truly loved, a great career, and friends who respected him. And he had confidence in himself, confidence that for so many years had evaded him, either because of naïveté or his continually faltering career. And he was finally able to admit it in public. "The big difference," he once mused, "is that when we were married the first time I was a little bit insecure in certain areas and jealous at times. The crew would be first and I would be second and I would get upset about that. It was just a matter of maturity and time going by."

This maturity brought with it responsible concern for the politics of the world and the imminent dangers that man was placing upon himself by tampering with the environment. R.J.'s love for the sea was now characterized by action. "I'm a great believer in Jacques Cousteau and his work. I want to get behind him as much as I can because what he's doing is so important. We take our waters for granted. We've changed the balance of nature and set off a chain reaction. But it's not too late. If we want to, we can put it all back and set the balance straight again. We've just got to make the attempt."

R.J. and Natalie worked together on the pollution problem.

Watching their children grow, they wanted them to be able to experience life on the water. Their kids influenced so much of what they did. They loved them, and from them they got the kind of support that makes for a balanced and pleasantly sane life. Despite this serenity, rumors cropped up that their marriage was shaky. Such innuendo can be very trying on a marriage, no matter how happy the couple is. It's a constant irritant, something that can cause guilt and jealousy, especially between two such public figures. If the rumors persist, they can undermine the all-important will of the two people to hold the marriage together. Once the will is gone, a marriage is defenseless against its predators. It's no surprise, then, that the Wagners despised these rumors and any who might be spreading them. Their marriage had already failed once, and each had had another failed marriage.

In 1977, when the British weekly *Reveille* published several articles alleging the couple's intent to divorce again, the Wagners had had enough, and they decided to do something about it. Not that *Reveille* was the only magazine hinting at an imminent dissolution of their marriage; it was simply the most brazen. Natalie and R.J. filed suit in London for libel. A year later, the Wagners won their case and (undisclosed) substantial damages to boot. "We are very happily married," R.J. insisted after the trial was over. They had just gone to a lot of trouble to prove it.

"I'm a very lucky guy," R.J. would often state, and he meant it. Once, in front of a reporter, he turned to Natalie and said, "You know, you look terrific. You've been working so hard but you look great!" Whereupon Natalie, very much pleased, returned, "You know, R.J., you've got a way with you," as she batted those wondrous big brown eyes at him.

He often went on about how pretty Natalie was despite the years. "Someone showed me a picture of her the other day taken twenty years ago. And do you know something? Natalie looks exactly the same today. Just great. I'm really a lucky fellow," he said. "I don't really work that hard at making it romantic because

Natalie can be so romantic anyway. I'm so in love with her, so it's just a matter of surprising her sometimes or doing things we like to do together.

"I don't really work at it too hard because it's kind of easy. I'm hooked on the lady, you see."

"I think we are a dream couple," Natalie added, "because we do have all these things going for us. We've been so lucky, so fortunate. You don't want to tamper with that too much.

"I have to pinch myself once in a while and say, 'My God, how lucky I am that it has all worked out, that it's all happened.' "

R.J.'s happiness and maturity allowed him finally to obtain the level of appreciation of life that he had always been striving for. He had overcome the intellectual tail-chasing. "I've learned to enjoy those special moments in life instead of thinking about how to enjoy them," he professed and, forgetting himself in his satisfaction, said again, "I'm a lucky man."

Natalie looked up at him. "We're lucky people," she said.

"We have each other," said R.J.

=21=

November 29, 1981

Toward 1:30 A.M. on Monday, November 29, 1981, aboard the *Splendour*, anchored just off Santa Catalina Island, R.J. walked down to Natalie's sleeping quarters to kiss her good night. He discovered she was not there.

"I wasn't alarmed," he says. "I casually went looking for her throughout the boat. During my search for her, I noticed the dinghy was missing. I thought perhaps she had gotten moody and gone to shore, though that wasn't at all like her. The idea that any harm had come to her never entered my mind. I got into my speedboat and went to look for her near the shore. I couldn't find her or the dinghy, and then I became worried after returning to the yacht and discovering she hadn't returned."

After phoning the restaurant where the two of them and actor Christopher Walken had dined that night, and finding she was not there either, R.J. called the harbor patrol. Five hours later, he received the tragic news of Natalie's drowning. She had been found at 7:45 A.M. more than a mile from the yacht, floating face down near Blue Cavern Point, wearing a blue nightgown, heavy woolen socks, and a red parka. The motorized dinghy, *Prince Valiant,* had not been started. It was beached nearby, its oars tied down.

The festive evening had been spent mostly at Doug's Harbor Reef, a casual restaurant located near the beach on isolated northern Catalina, where many yachtsman like to berth their boats. Conch shells, driftwood, and other beach motif trappings cluttered the dining room filled with bamboo and wicker chairs, palm trees, and fake ocean scenery. Accordion-player Jack Wright played Irish jigs. It was not the Plaza, but it was the only restaurant on that part of the island. R.J., Natalie, Chris Walken, and Dennis Davern, *Splendour*'s skipper, ate a late dinner, drank wine and champagne. Their table was very much the center of attention. In fact, several bottles of domestic Korbel Brut champagne were sent to them by the restaurant's admiring clientele. There was a lot of loud talk between Christopher Walken and R.J. The papers would take notice of that. Walken, Natalie's co-star in the yet unfinished movie *Brainstorm,* was the Wagners' guest for the long Thanksgiving weekend and was onboard *Splendour* when the accident occurred.

During dinner, they were approached by a young girl who wanted all of their autographs. Natalie, sitting in the corner in a big wicker chair, at once exhibited her sweet mothering tendencies. Says the restaurant's night manager, Don Whiting, "Natalie stunned everybody by taking the girl's hair. She began to braid it with a rubber band."

At 10:30 they paid their $65 check, leaving a $35 tip, and got up to leave. Walken hurled his champagne glass against the wall. It was a display of ritual bravura. R.J. followed his lead. Then Natalie threw her glass. The party was becoming rowdy. The accordian player tried to quiet the group by playing "Somewhere My Love." They'd had a good time, perhaps too good a time. Night manager Whiting thought it a good idea to watch them out the door and down the rain-slickened stairs. Then he called the harbor patrol and requested they see to it that the group make it back to the *Splendour.*

The newspapers made much of the event, and there was a good deal of speculation as to what might have provoked Natalie to go near the chilly water, of which she was self-confessedly very afraid, to try to get into the dinghy. What about the bottle of wine that was found in the dinghy? And the pills found next to her bed?

The first report to the public by the coroner's office, headed by the famous and controversial Dr. Thomas Noguchi (known as the real-life Quincy), elicited much media speculation. Issued the day after the discovery of her body, it caused a sensation in Hollywood circles as well. The report stated that there had been a "nonviolent argument" between Walken, Natalie's screen lover, and R.J. The report went on to say that the "fight" continued back aboard the yacht and that at a certain point Natalie became disgusted and stormed out of the room saying, "I've had enough."

Noguchi maintained that, already clad in her nightgown and parka, and still rather tipsy from the evening's debaucherie, Natalie went outside and walked to the stern of the yacht, where the dinghy was tethered. Upon trying to get into the dinghy, she slipped on the swim step and fell into the water, hitting her head on the side of the yacht. The bruises on her body and scrape on the side of her face, Noguchi felt, were consistent with this theory. He concluded that she may have struggled for a while but that the weight of her water-soaked clothes—the parka alone was thirty to forty pounds—and her state of intoxication—.04 percent over the legal driving limit—had been too much for her to be able to save herself. "It was quite possible she may have been yelling, but no one heard," Noguchi said. But this was strange, since *Prince Valiant*'s motor never had been started. There was no other noise to hear. Or was there? It was reported that a party on shore was blaring music across the water, and the howling wind and the rain were factors as well.

Noguchi summarized the report at a news conference by saying that Natalie's state of intoxication alone could not be blamed for the accident. Intoxication, however, was "one of the factors involved in the fact that she was not able to respond to the emergency." At the mention of the intoxication, the conference room erupted in a din of excitement. Reporters got their scoop. Already under fire for having blamed William Holden's death on the effects of alcohol, Noguchi decided not to mention the obvious: that though Natalie's body was found to contain a level above the state driving limit, the level when she had first fallen in the water, before struggling, had to have been much higher.

Noguchi stated finally, and, he hoped, with lasting resonance, that "there was no evidence of foul play. It was not a homicide. It was not a suicide. It was an accident."

Hollywood, nevertheless, was rife with rumors. What had the fight been about? Was it over Natalie? The coroner's office thought not. Said Assistant Coroner Richard Wilson, "They were arguing for general purposes. We don't know exactly why. There was no physical altercation. Each of the two gentlemen were examined. . . . She felt no danger at all. The argument was not over her." Some newspapers desperately tried to make it seem so, anyway. Outside the press, even nastier rumors began to circulate that R.J. and Walken were lovers and that theirs had been a lover's spat. Or, indeed, that theirs had been a singularly kinky relationship that also included Natalie. At the press conference, Noguchi said it might be useful to perform a "psychological autopsy" to find out why Natalie wanted to get away from the two of them.

The tabloids did all they could to fan the fire. Articles replete with uncorroborated reports of the alleged fight appeared all over the country. Reporters frantically called the Wagner residence vainly hoping to get an interview, a word, anything at all. R.J., however, was devastated by his loss, and he was not talking to anyone. His friends were keeping the reporters, as well as the circulating rumors, from him. Indeed, it was said that R.J. was truly unable to talk about any aspect of the accident. Warren Cowan, a press agent and a close family friend, said, "I would say that chances of his discussing the incident are totally zero. He's just totally devastated by this." So the press latched onto Walken. It was reported that he had broken down in tears in the lobby of the Beverly Wilshire Hotel, where he was staying, upon reading the newspaper accounts of Natalie's death. When asked to comment on the affair, he couldn't talk. "I really don't think it is the time to talk about it now," he said. Why not? wondered the press. Looking haggard and gaunt, he refused to comment on whether or not there had been a fight. "I don't remember the coroner being there," he said of Dr. Noguchi's report.

The press termed his remarks bitter, his reticence and antagonistic manner a sign of guilt. Walken then decided to hole up in his hotel. He called his wife in New York and she flew out to help him. Things were getting out of hand.

"I think the important thing is that Dr. Noguchi concluded that it was an accidental drowning. That is precisely what we always felt, and, frankly, I don't see the relevance of some of the other things," said Paul Ziffren, the Wagners' attorney and close friend. "Obviously there can be all kinds of rumors and gossip, but as far as I'm concerned the only significant thing is that she is gone. It's a terrible waste and the whys and the wherefores at this point are irrelevant."

Commenting on the reason why Natalie left the boat, George Kirvay, another close friend, thought that Natalie grew tired of listening to the men argue and decided to get some fresh air on the *Prince Valiant:* "I know when R.J. and I would get into long arguments at their home, Natalie would get bored and just wander away," he recalled.

The possibility of suicide was brushed aside by everyone interviewed. Thomas Thompson, who wrote the stage version of *Anastasia* planned as Natalie's stage debut at the Ahmanson Theatre in Los Angeles in two months' time, considered suicide "impossible. If I were casting that part, Natalie Wood would have been the last person in the world I'd have cast. She had a sensational life with R.J. and they were so mushy and goo-goo it used to embarass me when we were out together. She was a wonderful mother." He added that her career, after relinquishing it for five years for motherhood, "was just exploding" at that time.

It was also the consensus of all those interviewed that neither Natalie nor R.J. were big drinkers. Thompson said, "I've known her twenty years and I've never seen her take a drink of whiskey or anything else." Just reasonable amounts of white wine, "as most civilized people do." Of course, he had to be covering up for

Natalie and R.J. Either that or he was never around when Natalie happened to be getting tipsy. Several years before her death, Natalie had started drinking regularly, sometimes heavily, at parties. Still, the amount of alcohol that Natalie had consumed over the years was not relevant to her death. "What this was," Thompson continued emotionally, "was a bloody, stupid accident. We all have a fragile grip on life and Natalie just lost it."

The police wanted the whole incident put to rest once and for all. They questioned R.J. and Walken, as well as the witnesses, about the exact nature of the fight. Their findings argued against there having been a serious fight. Investigator Roy Hamilton said, "I don't know where the coroner got that information. We talked to Wagner and Walken and there was no indication that there was any argument. I think he [Noguchi] was juicing it up a little bit." Noguchi said that Assistant Coroner Wilson had been led by the police to give validity to the notion of an argument.

On December 2, the day after R.J. and Walken were interviewed and the day Natalie was buried, Noguchi's office released a statement of retraction. Assistant Coroner Wilson said, "We think 'argument' might be too strong a word. It might have been an animated conversation, heated conversation, a lot of conversation over a period of hours." Further, it was stated that the bottle of wine that had been found was one that the group had wanted to take to the restaurant but forgotten. Indeed, they did take two other bottles into the restaurant with them.

This statement did not allay the rumors. Many around Hollywood were beginning to talk about a cover-up. It had been discovered that two days before the ill-fated dinner, Natalie had checked into the Pavilion Lodge on Catalina Island without R.J. "She looked like she was a little down, kind of depressed," said Paul Morrell, a hotel employee. In people's minds, something was lacking in the case. Then it came out that Walken had checked into the same hotel the same night. But these reports were incorrect; it was later disclosed that the other man had been *Splendour* skipper Dennis Davern. Davern was at the lodge apparently to console Natalie. When he finally broke his silence in June 1985, four years after the accident, Davern told reporter Brian Haugh that throughout the weekend "Natalie was [already] being very flirtatious with Walken."

On Friday night, when Natalie and Walken talked exclusively about *Brainstorm*, R.J. decided he wanted to move the *Splendour*. That's why, according to Davern, Natalie went ashore Friday night. She returned to the boat on Saturday, and then she and Walken took the dinghy ashore alone. Later, R.J. and Davern joined them for drinks at Doug's Harbor Reef. The drinking intensified Natalie's flirting with Walken, said Davern, which in turn exacerbated R.J.'s jealousy.

The last evening Natalie was alive was marked by harsh words between her and R.J. When they returned to the yacht at 11:00 P.M., "Natalie lit some candles on the coffee table in the salon room and she and Chris sat together on a small couch, sort of a love seat," Davern recalled.

"I was sitting across the table from them and R.J. was standing, glaring at them. Natalie was still flirting with Chris, hugging him and holding his arm. And Walken was doing nothing to discourage her.

"R.J. got redder and redder in the face and finally exploded. He picked up a bottle of wine and smashed it on the table in front of Walken. 'What are you trying to do, seduce my wife?' he shouted at Walken."

According to Davern, Natalie was incensed. "R.J., I won't stand for this," she said.

Those were the last words she spoke to R.J.

22

Balalaika Dirge

While Hollywood was boiling over with the added heat, R.J. was secluded in his home. Except for the interview with the police, no one (especially the press) had been allowed anywhere near him. Of course, his immediate family and closest friends sat with him, but he was extremely morose. These were silent times. He was described as being distraught and in "total shock." R.J. remained in his bedroom, suffering and crying. "R.J. is not doing well at all," said a close friend who requested anonymity. R.J. even refused to see any of the notables who were calling him to express their condolences, including Elizabeth Taylor, who felt it was her duty to succor him in his hour of need. The newspapers loved this, and wondered if it were actually possible that Elizabeth Taylor and R.J. could be romantically involved.

R.J. was wondering something else. His musings ate at his heart. Could it be possible that he had again lost Natalie? Why had this happened to him, just when everything was right? Just when he was the happiest he had ever been? As these thoughts, so crushingly real, circulated in his stunned mind, he had to prepare for the funeral.

The actual arrangements for the funeral were made by a close friend of the family. R.J. was too grief-stricken to assume full responsibility for the onerous task. It was to be a small and private affair. Only relatives and close friends were invited. There was to be none of the glamorous hoopla that had surrounded Natalie, once known as the "Little Princess," for most of her life. The press was purposely excluded. Yet, though the time and place were kept secret, reporters and photographers managed to be in the right place at the right time.

On Wednesday, December 2, guards ringed the high walls circling the grounds of Westwood Memorial Park in Beverly Hills. Fifty reporters and photographers milled about outside. Everyone was tense. At around two o'clock, the limousines suddenly started to arrive. The gates were opened for them and them alone. The press grumbled. R.J. passed through in a blue limousine, and the cameras clicked furiously. With him were the three girls. On one side was Kate, now seventeen; on the other, Courtney, seven; Natasha, eleven, was sitting on R.J.'s lap. The car wended its way through the grounds, past the graves of many other stars, including the tomb of Marilyn Monroe, just one of the "unknowns" R.J. had screen-tested with. It came to a stop near a group of waiting mourners. The photographers and reporters fought the high wall for a better view.

Laurence Olivier, Gregory Peck, Frank Sinatra, Fred Astaire, Rock Hudson, Christopher Walken and his wife, and Stefanie Powers were already present at the side of the grave. It may not have had the fanfare associated with Natalie Wood—indeed, the mood was very somber—but it was certainly a star-studded affair. Stepping out of the car, R.J. shook hands with many of the mourners and then took his place front and center of the two short rows of chairs set up for family and friends. The cameras, clicking wildly, could be heard in the distance. Natasha was crying. Sitting on her nanny's lap, she wiped away the tears with a white lace handkerchief.

In the background, soft Russian balalaika music wafted through the air. It was a nice touch, and Natalie would have appreciated it, loving her Russian heritage as she had. Then, some distance away at the entrance to the chapel, borne on the shoulders of eight pallbearers, including Tom Mankiewicz and Mart Crowley, the gold-colored coffin appeared. Slowly, they walked toward the grave. Tears began to well up in R.J.'s eyes. Quiet sobbing could be heard from several of the mourners. They had lost the sparkle and the charm that was Natalie Wood, the flirty gamin who could win her way with those big brown eyes. For R.J., the loss was also of the woman who had provided him with inconceivable joy and happiness for the last nine years. It was the loss of love renewed, which is the best love of all because of its confidence and sincerity. Having already lost her once, the all too familiar pain clashed with the unbounded joy of just a few days before and doubled his grief. This time it was not Warren Beatty but life itself that was cheating him. The pallbearers approached and set the closed casket down.

The Reverend Stephen Fitzgerald of the Russian Orthodox Church of the Holy Virgin Mary in North Hollywood officiated at the quick service. Roddy McDowall, Hope Lange, and Thomas Thompson delivered emotionally fraught eulogies. "She found not only a way to put life into her art, but art into her life," McDowall said. Natalie was a "pillar of strength for us all," said Lange.

Getting ready to leave, a sobbing R.J. bent over to kiss the coffin. The cameras flew into a rage. From the lilies draped over the coffin R.J. picked three and gave one to each of the girls. He then led the family, forever reduced by one, back to the waiting limousine. They whisked through the gates back to his mansion. The whole thing had lasted a mere fifteen minutes.

Ten minutes later, after everyone had left, Natalie's coffin was lowered into its grave and covered with earth. Several days later, a stone monument saying simply, "Wagner-Wood" was unveiled.

After the funeral, R.J. went straight into his bedroom again and shut the world out. "It's like he thinks someone made a horrible mistake and Natalie will just come walking in the door anytime," said his friend *Daily Variety* columnist Army Archerd, who was at the house after the service. "I think he looks on it as a bad movie that needs a retake," said Lionel Stander. "He's just shattered. He'll survive, but he'll never forget." At home, it was said that R.J. could only sit and stare out the window, occasionally burying his face in his hands.

The rumors and innuendos continued to swirl through the Hollywood gossip lines and into the newspapers. Yet, the stories had become much less malevolent. No doubt the gossip mongers had begun to see reason. Well, perhaps not entirely. Now they talked about how Natalie was doomed to die because of her involvement with the movie *Rebel Without a Cause*. Both her co-stars in that movie had come to a violent end, James Dean smashing up his car and Sal Mineo being knifed in a parking lot. There was also talk of jinxes stalking the "Hart to Hart" show, Stefanie Powers having just lost William Holden.

Perhaps Natalie's will had something to do with the decreasing virulence. It left no doubt that she must have trusted R.J. in every way. Read two days after the funeral, it specified that Wagner was to be executor and trustee of the will, which was dated April 17, 1980. The bulk of her estate, estimated to be in the millions, but termed in the will as being in "excess of $10,000," was to be divided among her two daughters, Natasha and Courtney, and R.J. The portions were to be roughly equal. To Kate, Natalie left one-tenth or $50,000, whichever was less, of the children's estate. To Lana Wood, her actress sister, she left her furs and clothing. To Olga Viripaeff, her half-sister, she left $15,000. Natalie also saw to it that her mother, Maria Gurdin of Los Angeles, would receive $7,500 to $12,000 a year from income earned by the children's trust. Natalie's favorite painting, *The Three Stages of Motherhood,* by Bonnard, and another painting of similar value, to be chosen by R.J., were left to her two daughters. Other art, automobiles, furniture, and jewelry were left to R.J., who, according to the will, knew of Natalie's wishes that various items go to certain people.

All this surely proved that Natalie had great confidence in R.J. as a husband, a friend, and a lover. The most telling sign of all, however, was Natalie's mandate that R.J. be named guardian of Natasha, her daughter from her marriage to British producer Richard Gregson. Natalie wanted, as the will stated, that her two daughters continue to live together as they had for most of their lives. "The best interests of my daughter Natasha would be served if [R.J.] were appointed guardian," she said in her will. So as not to precipitate a tremendous dispute about the matter, though, she further specified that Gregson, if he wished, could have custody of Natasha after all. "My husband has assured me he would cooperate with Natasha's father in the same manner I would cooperate with him," she wrote in her will. It can not be denied that Natalie believed in her heart that R.J. was as good and true a husband and a father as she could hope for.

Natalie must have had tremendous confidence in her house-keeper, Willie Mae Worthen, as well. If R.J. were to die before the children had grown, the will specified that they be remanded to her custody.

On the same day the will was read, it was discovered that someone may have heard Natalie crying for help the night that she drowned. It appears that for almost a half an hour she yelled, "Help me! Somebody help me!" This fact was reported by stock-broker Marylin Wayne. Ms. Wayne was on a yacht not 150 feet away from *Splendour* the night Natalie drowned. She heard the cries but thought someone else would eventually rescue the victim because of answering shouts of "We're coming to get you" ema-nating from one of the neighboring boats. There were eighty or so boats in the harbor that night and there was a party on one. It sounded to Wayne as if the cries and answers were coming from the one with the party. "What a terrible tragedy," mused Ms. Wayne; "Natalie Wood could have been saved." Perhaps. But it is impossible to be sure whose cries they really were and what they were about. Predictably, the papers wondered why neither R.J., Walken, nor Davern, who were all awake at the time, had heard the cries.

A month later, when R.J. could finally talk about the incident, he gave his version of the events of the evening through a close friend; he still refused to talk to reporters. Quoting Wagner, his friend said: "We reached the boat in a happy frame of mind after spending a few hours at the restaurant eating and drinking. During dinner, I got into a political debate with Walken and we continued it aboard the yacht. There was no fight, no anger. Just a lot of words thrown around like you hear in most political discussions such as 'you don't know what you're talking about!' Natalie sat there not saying much of anything and looking bored. She left us after about a half hour, and we sat there talking for almost another hour. Then I went down to kiss her good night, and found her missing."

R.J. believes that Natalie never wanted to leave the yacht. Instead, he thinks that she could not sleep because the *Prince Valiant,* poorly tethered, kept on knocking into the side of the yacht. R.J. continued: "It was only after I was told that she was dressed in a sleeping gown, heavy socks, and a parka that it dawned on me what had really occurred. Natalie obviously had trouble sleeping with that dinghy slamming up against the boat. It happened many, many times before, and I had always gone out and pulled the ropes tighter to keep the dinghy flush against the yacht.

"She probably skidded on one of the steps after untying the ropes. The steps are slick as ice because of the algae and seaweed that's always clinging to them.

"After slipping on the steps, she hit her head against the boat. . . . I only hope she was unconscious when she hit the water."

Since R.J. was bitter over the treatment of the case in the newspapers and, indeed, had not read many of the reports, he did not know that it is probable that Natalie was awake when she hit the water and that she struggled for quite a long time to save her life. Two years after the tragedy, Dr. Noguchi published a book, *Coroner,* in which he confirmed the belief that Natalie was not knocked out upon hitting the side of the boat. In fact, Noguchi believes that, had she been able to remove her water-laden parka, she might have lived. "Natalie Wood fought for her life in that cold November ocean," he says. "She did not give up. Instead, she began to perform a feat that was both unique and gallant. And she almost achieved a miracle."

Noguchi's deputy, Paul Miller, an ocean accidents specialist who happened to be in another boat right near R.J.'s the night of Natalie's drowning, understood that Natalie had come very close to saving herself. He told his boss. Agreeing with R.J.'s theory, Noguchi and Miller believed that on that very windy night, Natalie had probably wanted to stop the dinghy from banging against the yacht. Though the dinghy was made of rubber and was soft, its sound was amplified inside the hull. As she untethered the boat, she stumbled into the water. Coming up for air, she grabbed the dinghy to stabilize herself. She probably thought she was safe; the yacht was only feet away. Because of the location of the island, the wind naturally blows east toward the California mainland thirty miles away, and that night it was blowing very hard. Before she knew it, Natalie was a great distance from the yacht, making re-entry by way of the swim step impossible. Her cries for help, though heard at first, quickly became inaudible because of the loud music. Though Noguchi does not say so, it is also very hard to hear someone downwind.

Natalie struggled to get into the boat but the sides of the *Valiant,* large and round, gave her no possibility for leverage. This was verified by the fact that Miller found numerous fingernail scratches on the side of the boat. It is thought that she maneuvered her way to the stern of the *Valiant* and tried a sailor's trick for getting over the side by facing away from the boat, putting her arm around the engine, and pushing herself up using the ring around the propeller. This would explain some of the bruises that were found on her lower legs. Lifting herself up, she must have felt a great weight pulling her back down. This was her red parka, laden with water.

Not thinking enough to take her parka off, she came up with another idea remarkable for its ingenuity. Though the wind blew out toward the mainland in the east, Blue Point Cavern lies almost due south of where the yachts were anchored. Though no one thought to mention it, it was strange that Natalie should have ended up there. As it turns out, a current of one knot flows toward the cavern despite the wind. Natalie must have tried to take advantage of it and spent hours paddling the boat in that direction. She could not have arrived there by being blown there. Beyond a certain point, she could not have been blown back out from there because there's no wind in the immediate vicinity of the cavern. The fact that she was found only a little way from the shore must mean that that is exactly where she succumbed to exhaustion and hypothermia. The *Valiant,* lighter and riding right on top of the water but away from the wind, would have still been influenced by the current, which explains why it made it to shore— probably only minutes after Natalie let go of it.

All the theories and hypotheses wouldn't change the fact that Natalie was gone. The perfect mariage had ended—again, and this time for good. Friends and fans mourned its passing. The dream couple who had everything was gone. R.J. had suffered so many problems in his life, and it must have seemed that fate was truly his enemy. The search for happiness—that happiness that he had finally known firsthand but had irretrievably lost—would have to begin again. But how could it ever be the same? It couldn't. And that demon fact would live with R.J. for the rest of his life.

23
Picking Up the Pieces

R.J. lay despondent upon his bed for days. Today, recalling his emotional anguish, he speaks in a quiet voice. "Losing someone you love so suddenly, so tragically," he says, pausing, "you feel like you're going to hit bottom. It's the deepest depression you can ever know."

At the sight of R.J. languishing in despair, the Wagners' housekeeper, Willie Mae Worthen, began to wonder if the family was ever going to pull itself together again. Certainly, Mr. Wagner, she thought, wasn't making any signs of recovery, just lying there in his bedroom. Who was going to give these poor kids the support that they need?

Indeed, since Natalie's drowning, it was the girls who were giving support to R.J. They had been the ones to say that there was still enough love for them all to be able to go on, and they were showing him that it was true by giving him all the love they had. It was the girls who were saving the sinking ship. "Maybe the only reason I could handle it at all was because I wasn't alone," R.J. recalls. "I didn't have much strength in the beginning. But the strength I felt from the children was incredible. I honestly think they comforted me more than I comforted them." Kate, R.J.'s first daughter, who was seventeen when her stepmother drowned, "helped me so much through the terrible time after I lost Natalie," he says.

The first weekend after Natalie's death arrived, and all of them were very despondent, coming to grips with the fact that Natalie would not be there. Willie Mae saw that she would have to do something. She couldn't be the one to tell the kids to go back to school; Mr. Wagner would have to do that. But she could tell Mr. Wagner to pull himself together.

She went into R.J.'s bedroom. Cautiously, but with determination, she told R.J. that it was time to pick up the pieces and move on. The children needed his help and strength. He had to put aside his mourning now, for if it went on much longer it wouldn't be anything more than selfishness. "I couldn't get out of bed because I was absolutely devastated. And this wonderful woman who works for us, who has been with our family for a long time, said, 'Mr. Wagner, you've just got to get up—for the kids. You can't have them just lying there.' " So R.J. got up and went to talk to the girls. He was determined to do the right thing by them.

Seeing them, he knew he had love. But he also saw a searching look in their eyes, a what-are-we-going-to-do-now look. He understood it was time for him to give back the love they had given him. It was time to become a father to them again. "I had such a responsibility to the kids," he says with a tinge of awe.

At first, he exercised that responsibility in a very Hollywood way. Immediately after Natalie's death, R.J. made appointments for Natasha and Courtney to see a child psychologist. "The one thing I didn't want to happen was for my girls to become emotionally crushed by the loss of this wonderful woman who had great humor and was loving and everything else you could wish for. I wanted them to let out all their anger and frustration, all their feelings of pain and loss and confusion, so they could start to accept it and live a new life. I wanted them to realize it wasn't the end. I wanted a way of monitoring them so they could survive this and come through it okay. The important thing was to get help. They'll never get over the emotional loss; but they may accept it on terms they can handle." Next, he made an appointment for himself to return to therapy.

Two days later, R.J. was able to summon up enough courage to give a very necessary, yet painful command. On Monday, just seven days after the tragedy, R.J. gave the order to sell the *Splendour*.

They had been remarried on that yacht. It was the symbol of their new beginning. It was their favorite home away from home. Now it was synonymous with their end. R.J. had loved the ocean, the peace and solitude it offered. It had been a haven away from the goldfish bowl life he led back on terra firma. But now would R.J. ever go near the water again?

Not for a while anyway, even though the goldfish spotters were more intent than ever and would remain that way for months to come. Across the street from R.J.'s house there seemed to be a permanent encampment of photographers, while many tourists, alone and in tour buses, gawked all day long. A new security system was ordered.

That Saturday after Willie Mae talked to him R.J. announced to the world that he would go back to work the following Wednesday. Sure enough, just nine days after Natalie's drowning, he was back on the set of "Hart to Hart" to film "Heart of Diamonds," an episode about a kleptomaniac. It was not that he so much wanted to go back, it's that he needed to. From now on his life would become a second-by-second grind. Plunging himself back into work was the only way R.J. was going to make it through the days with his sanity intact.

The press was astounded. Hollywood was aghast. How could R.J. be back to work so soon? They thought the series was going to be cancelled; that, by all accounts, R.J. was truly devastated by Natalie's drowning, his state of shock being so total that he could not possibly resume work in the near future. Everyone knew he was a workaholic, but this was unbelievable. Besides, the show was four weeks ahead of schedule. In response to the press queries, R.J. said simply, but truthfully, "I can't very well tell my children to go to school while I sit locked up in my room crying." How else could he be a father if he was not doing what his children had always known and expected him to do?

It is a testament to R.J.'s willpower that he was able to cope with what must have been extremely trying days back at work. He did, however, have Stefanie Powers there to help him. In fact, they exchanged emotional support. Stephanie had recently lost her lover William Holden. Since she and R.J. shared the same feelings, they knew how to console each other. "We are a big happy family in 'Hart to Hart,'" Stephanie said, "and when double tragedy struck we were bonded together. Robert and I were a great help to each other," she continued. "It would have been very hard to get through otherwise. We found solace working in 'Hart to Hart,' and we had the strength to pull through. It was a rough time for both of us."

Because the press and the public knows no moderation, the set was declared off-limits to anyone but those actually involved in the shooting. "It's tough enough as it is and we don't want it any worse," said an ABC representative the day R.J. went back to work. "Since Natalie's death, there have been people camping out on the lawn of his home trying to snap his picture, and we're trying to avoid the same thing happening at the studio. You'd be amazed at the requests we've gotten, particularly from the foreign press, to do photo coverage of Wagner's first day back on the series." During the series hiatus that was soon to come, R.J. would also manage to bury his grief by filming two movies, *I Am the Cheese* and *The Trail of the Pink Panther*.

While Hollywood was still recovering from the shocker of his speedy return to "Hart to Hart," R.J. decided that the Christmas holidays couldn't possibly be spent on Canon Drive, at the home he and Natalie had lived in since their remarriage seven years earlier. Natalie's ghost hung over the place like a shroud of sadness. From every nook and cranny of the house she had so lovingly decorated, her presence—or rather, her absence—could be felt. It was a torture to everyone in the family. This Christmas could not be expected to be a terribly happy one. Even if they'd decorated a tree, it would sit in the room where Natalie delighted in breast-feeding Courtney. The memories were too sad. The holiday was doomed before it even began. To escape, R.J. decided to take the family to Gstaad, Switzerland, for a month-long ski vacation. For the kids it was a treat to get away from the house. What with the photographers and tourists always hanging about the place, the Canon Drive place had become more of a prison than a home. Gstaad, however, did not turn out to be all that private either. Natalie's tragic death had piqued Europe's interest at least as much as America's. And of course there were those American photographers who make their living out of following celebrities wherever they might go. After all, Gstaad was not the outback.

Photographers were everywhere. When the family hit the slopes, shutterbugs would be hanging out of trees or running into the Wagner clan, letting the perfect camera angle become more important than turning their skis—if they knew how to turn them. The Wagners' vacation was fun enough, though, even as they tried to concentrate on getting over their grief.

When they got home, the oglers across the street were still there, but now the family was strong enough to live with them, at least for a while.

Though no one, not even R.J., knew it at the time, he would soon again unwittingly shock Hollywood. In fact, the seeds for what was to come had been planted even before he left for Switzerland.

While he was lying on his bed that dismal week after Natalie's drowning, one person did manage to see him briefly. Two years younger than Natalie, a one-time ballet classmate of hers, Jill St. John, a 1950s sex symbol, stopped by to offer her condolences. She'd known R.J. since they were both just beginning their careers as contract players with 20th Century–Fox. Later she starred as R.J.'s love interest in *Banning* and was featured in the pilot for "Hart to Hart," as a character who was killed off. Although she denies making the first move, Jill freely admits that she wanted to see R.J. She sent flowers to him the day after Natalie died. He never received them, however, because he'd asked that all gifts and flowers be sent to nearby Children's Hospital. That didn't matter, though, as Jill had also asked Tom Mankiewicz, her boyfriend at the time and creative consultant on "Hart to Hart," to bring them together somehow. "When Natalie passed away," said Jill, "I told Tom that I would like to see R.J. sometime, to tell him how badly I felt for him and to ask if I could help in any way. About a week later Tom took me over to R.J.'s house to see him, and we talked for about forty-five minutes. Then I didn't see R.J. again. I didn't call him and he didn't call me."

For reasons that are not clear, about two months after the initial encounter, Mankiewicz decided to get Jill together with R.J. again. Inviting Jill to dinner, Mankiewicz asked R.J. and Kate to join them. "We had a good time at dinner," recalled Jill, "and the next day R.J. called and asked me out. I was surprised because we'd known each other for so long, and there was never any hint of romance, only really good friendship. So I thought about it for a while, and I decided, yes, I really liked him a lot and I should see him. We started seeing each other, and neither of us has dated anyone else since."

Feminine wiles accounted for part of Jill's success with R.J. "I know a lot of women did go after him and are still doing so," Jill said. "When I see women coming on to him, I sort of smile because that's the kind of woman he dislikes the most. In fact, I really think that had I 'gone after him,' it wouldn't have worked." In fact, more than twenty years earlier, R.J. had decided he "didn't even like girls to phone me," as he said then. "That's okay for an old friend, but not someone I've just met. Agressive gals leave me cold."

Though they became very close, he and Jill remained independent, keeping separate residences in the years following Natalie's death. "I'm so self-sufficient I don't think of myself as needing protection," Jill said soon after they got together.

Their relationship was never kept a secret, but, due to R.J.'s lingering need for seclusion, the press was slow to pick up on it. First, when it was thought Jill might star on an episode of "Hart to Hart," she was termed his good friend. Then they were seen dining out together. They left quickly. After a while, the rumors began to fly. Has R.J. found a new love? They were spotted again somewhere else. It's happening, the press thought; they are definitely more than just friends. Slowly, Jill went from being friend to new love.

With little provocation, the press decided that R.J. and Jill were going to get married. The only detail the press lacked was when. This did not please R.J. It made him feel as though he were being railroaded into marriage. R.J. was not amused. It wasn't at his own speed. Jill was certainly very attractive and, indeed, available. And he needed her. What he didn't need was the extra tension the press was creating.

How could R.J. start a relationship so soon after Natalie's death, Hollywood wanted to know. "I don't like solitude," he said thoughtfully. "I get anxious when I'm alone." To others he has said, "I don't give a damn what anyone thinks." On a more philosophical note, he added, "Everybody's been hurt. Everybody's been knocked down. But you have to remain open to life. You can't see very much if your eyes are always clouded with tears.

"I'm a positive person," he continued. "I'm a romantic. It's true that romantics can get crushed. Everyone has had loss. It's the way you put the pieces back together that counts."

Several months after the courtship between Jill and R.J. began, Rudy Diaz, a supporting actor who played a small part on "Hart to Hart," said, "I've known R.J. since he was sixteen years old. He was a happy-go-lucky kid then, and he hasn't changed a bit."

"Well," R.J. responded, "I'm trying very hard not to. I think enthusiasm is the greatest thing you can have in life. Obviously, life has to go on. But it's very hard because before, with Natalie, I was living a wonderful life. It just flowed naturally and I didn't have to work at it. Now I'm trying to recreate that excitement." It may be his hardest role to date.

Said Jill, "If I could help a friend, and at the same time receive comfort myself, of a different kind . . . well, it's been very beneficial to both of us." Many times Jill has played substitute mother at certain functions, such as Kate's graduation from Beverly Hills High in June 1982, and on vacation trips. She recalls that when she first started seeing R.J., a woman warned her against it, saying that she would not want to be the one to take Natalie's place. "I'm not taking anyone's place," she retorted. "I make my own." She has not been afraid of being just a little bit outside his sphere of love.

When it comes to R.J., that sphere seems to grow larger, embracing more, every day.

24

The Menagerie

Imagine a brood of kids around a kitchen range. The grown man in their midst carefully flips a lamb chop, sprinkles a little rosemary on it, and smiles. The children laugh.

Scenes like this often took place in the Wagner household after Natalie died. R.J. tried to be at home with the girls as much as possible. Most of the time, he did the cooking: chicken, veal, fish, healthy things. "They think I'm one of the greatest cooks in the world," he said of his daughters. "That's our idea of a good time."

At that time, he became more of his old self again, and more than his old self. He restructured his relationship with his daughters so that they could accept him as both mother and father, so that they could feel confident in life. According to R.J., this task was made easy by Natalie's talent for being a wonderful and loving mother. "I was made a single father by a tremendous tragedy," R.J. said, his voice cracking. "But one thing I was very fortunate about was that Natalie was a great mother. It's just a matter of sustaining the goodness and love she put there. Thank God they had her as long as they did."

R.J. did everything humanly possible, short of quitting his acting career, to provide as normal and stable a life for the children as they had had when both parents were around.

After returning from Gstaad, he began coming out of seclusion more and more. Mostly, he would be found doing things with his kids. His first appearance was at the Golden Globe Awards in late January 1982. He took Kate with him for that one. Next, with

Courtney and Natasha, he took part in a celebrity softball game at Beverly Hills High. R.J. is never really far from his work, and that turned out to be the case in these first outings. The Golden Globe Awards, of course, are the equivalent of a business convention for movie stars. The softball game was business as well, a charity called "Play Ball for 'Hart to Hart,' " held to kick off the American Heart Association's National Heart Month. But there's no doubt he used these occasions to be near his children.

During this period, he flew to New York to film *I Am the Cheese* starring *E.T.* child actor Robert MacNaughton as an alienated youth who's witnessed his parents' death. "Everybody warned me to go easy with R.J.," MacNaughton recalled. " 'No shenanigans,' [director Robert] Jiras told me. I was on my best behavior and then R.J. arrived and cracked a couple of jokes. It turned out he put everyone at ease, not the other way around." R.J.'s only concern during filming was that the movie would wrap in time for him to attend Kate's graduation from Beverly Hills High. He flew home just in time, and after the ceremony was over, R.J. and Jill took Kate and fourteen of her classmates to lunch at the lovely Bistro Garden.

One of Kate's graduation gifts was a special father-daughter trip to London and Paris later that summer. R.J. had already been on a just-the-two-of-us adventure with Natasha in the spring, taking her to the south of France. Squeezed in between graduation day, June 18, and the start of "Hart to Hart" on June 28, was a trip with Courtney to Hawaii. He planned the trips with each of the girls individually so that each could have her own private moments with "Daddy." R.J. loves his daughters dearly, and his devotion to them and to fatherhood shone through very plainly during that period of sorrow. It was, after all, only for them that he got out of bed.

Gone before 6:00 A.M., working twelve to fourteen hours a day on the set of "Hart to Hart," R.J. realized that "every parent can't do everything. It's impossible, particularly for people who work. I was frequently gone before the kids went to school. But sometimes, if my call was later, I'd take them. If I was on location or at the studio, they'd come by and see me after school." Whenever he made a movie during that mourning period, he tried to take the children with him on location.

During the first year after Natalie's death, it became apparent that the house on Canon Drive was more a burden than a home. Not only could Natalie's touch be seen and felt everywhere, but the tourists never let up. "The children couldn't even go out the front door," R.J. said. "It was a nightmare."

Finding his new house took a bit of serendipity. Natasha had expressed a desire to own a horse, so in the spring of 1983, R.J. bought her a gelding named Fad-a-lei. "Natasha got me back into horses," says R.J., and, sure enough, soon after he bought the gelding for Natasha he bought himself two mares for $50,000 each. He needed a new hobby. "The sea no longer holds much attraction for me," he said. As for the *Splendour,* there were no buyers. R.J. eventually gave the boat to the Sea Scouts.

A month or so after purchasing the horses, R.J., Jill, Natasha, and Courtney were supposed to fly to upstate California to an Arabian horse ranch in Stockton, where R.J. was breeding his mares. The girls spent too long primping and fussing that morning and they all missed the plane. Instead, the whole gang piled into the car. Along the way, they passed a modified ranch house, which they immediately fell in love with. Amazingly, it had a For Sale sign on the front lawn. The kids became very excited and insisted that R.J. go investigate the possibility of purchasing the property. Soon after, R.J. closed the deal and became the proud and relieved owner of a place away from the Canon Drive oglers. He put the Canon Drive house on the market. His asking price? $2.9 million.

R.J. realized that this was an opportunity for him and the family to make a fresh start, to put distance between them and the pain they had suffered the last year. However, he also knew that it would be improper for him to refuse the girls some remembrances of the past. "I didn't want to take their mother away from them completely," he said. "So I told the girls they could take any furniture they wanted from the old house to keep in their rooms, and, if there was anything else they wanted, I would keep it in storage for them until they grow up. But," he continued with the resolve of a man who has accepted his fate, good or bad, "I think the time has come to turn a new page."

Other kids lived with R.J. as well. There was the gaiety of a sleep-over party every night. In addition to his own daughters, there were Marion Marshall's two sons, Josh Donen, then twenty-six, and Peter Donen, twenty-nine. Josh, now a producer (and once a paramour of Cher) who started as R.J.'s theatrical agent, helped relieve some of the tension of being without Natalie. "At first," R.J. said, "I didn't sleep at night unless my stepson [Josh] was in the house with me." Besides Josh and Peter, Richard Gregson's sons also dropped in a lot. Gregson and R.J. were getting along very well by then and would even discuss working together.

Set on four acres of undeveloped land, the West Los Angeles house had plenty of room for all the children. They began seriously riding horses, getting up early and grooming their steeds in the new stables. There was also a menagerie of pets populating the grounds, including four dogs, two cats, several goats (offspring of a goat presented them by Shaun Cassidy), and a hatch of cackling hens donated by Stefanie Powers with her usual sense of humor. The children took complete charge of the zoo. "It teaches them responsibility," R.J. said. Farm living, such as it was, was enhanced by a few luxuries on the grounds, including a pool and a paddle tennis court.

In these first years after Natalie was gone, the children led full lives, marked by a combination of privilege and the ordinary. R.J. even tried to help the kids with their homework, but like most parents, he was often embarassed to say he was sometimes confounded by the material they brought to him. In his effort to be a super-parent, he sometimes forgot the girls also had a life of their own. Occasionally, he smothered them, but even this, he realized, was better than not enough love.

During Christmas week 1982, the family, including Jill, went off to Gstaad again. This time R.J. brought along old friend and "Hart to Hart" producer Mart Crowley as well. R.J. had apparently come to terms with the ubiquitous presence of the paparazzi and had actually gone ahead and bought himself a Swiss chalet. "Gstaad," he said, "is just a marvelous, relaxing environment for us all." In his typically uncomplaining way he continued, "They hounded us terribly there the first time and it probably won't be much better. It bothered the girls a lot, but, well, I guess it just comes with the territory."

In January he flew to England to film two segments of "Hart to Hart." Over the objections of the girls' teachers, R.J. took them for the whole trip. This time, however, he would not commit himself to any movies during the "Hart to Hart" hiatus as he had the year before when made *I Am the Cheese* and *Trail of the Pink Panther.* "I won't do anything like that again," he said. "I just want to get away and rest, and devote my time to the girls. My life revolves around my work and my family. Every time I have a chance to show them something new and experience that through their eyes, I try to do it. To be able to give them that is a great advantage."

As any loving parent does, R.J. has made mistakes in raising his children. However, he tries hard to understand their problems. "I think one of the most important aspects of being a good father is to acknowledge your children's feelings. Whatever their problems are, you have to listen and understand without cutting them off or telling them 'later' because you don't think it's important. [The children] understand about my work, but they always know where I am."

And, thanks to R.J.'s efforts, his children know him deep-down as well.

25

Getting By

S everal years have passed since that cruel November night of Natalie's untimely death. And though it is said that time heals all wounds, R.J. can't forget his darling Natalie with the deepest of brown eyes. He often visits her grave, where, upon arriving, he is deferentially given his solitude by the two or three other visitors, strangers to R.J. but Natalie's most loyal fans, who pay their weekly respects. Placing a bouquet of roses at the foot of her grave, he may think for a moment of the many years that have come and gone since the day when, still a buildup boy in the Fox system, he met her and they fell in love. What have those years meant to him?

Caddying so long ago for Clark Gable and other "special" people who frequented the Beverly Hills Country Club, he dreamed of becoming a star himself, of experiencing being on top of the world. Well, in his many years in the movie business, he has learned all about that star stuff. And it is vividly apparent to him that the highest highs he will ever experience, as well as the lowest lows, are buried beneath the scattered flowers left on Natalie's grave by adoring fans. As he leaves, R.J. heads for a life apart from the past.

Since the dark early days without Natalie, R.J. has been able to bounce back from painful despair. Along the way a lot of people pitched in to help him. "It was a difficult time for me," he says, "and I am eternally grateful to my friends in the industry and the public for being so supportive. Without them, I couldn't have made it." Since then, aside from maintaining a fulfilling home life, he's occupied himself with a myriad of different projects, including the HBO movie *To Catch a King,* the story of a Nazi plan to kidnap the Duke and Duchess of Windsor. In the World War II saga, Wagner played a nightclub owner who tries to thwart the plan.

He's become a major-league producer with an exclusive deal with Columbia Pictures to produce and/or star in his own projects. He's recently bought the rights to Gerald Browne's *Hazard,* a thriller about a spy with ESP, and he hopes to develop it as a TV movie.

Besides his business commitments, R.J. also spends a great deal of time on charity work. His boundless energy and capacity for work confound the imagination. In a sense, he is lost in his work, perhaps the better to keep from thinking too much. But of course, he's always been a workaholic. Once it was a matter of survival. Then, when success came, it was a matter of maintaining the excitement. With Natalie's death, it has become both.

Sadly, however, tragedy has dogged R.J.'s footsteps. A couple of former schoolteachers, Linda Bloodworth-Thomason and her husband, Harry Thomason, came up with the idea for a series starring R.J. as a globe-trotting insurance investigator who spends as much time with his family in Virginia as he does on glamorous cases. "The time was right for a single-father show," said Harry Thomason, the co-producer along with his wife and R.J. on the "Lime Street" series that first aired in the summer of 1985. "And R.J. was, of course, a single parent himself. From the moment the pilot script got the okay from ABC, our main concern was casting. And casting R.J.'s two daughters was one of our most difficult tasks. We wanted natural actors, not robot kids."

Maia Brewton, the eight-year-old who plays the younger daughter, Margaret Ann Culver, in the series, was an easy choice. She lives in West Los Angeles and had had just enough acting experience (on series like "Trapper John, M.D." and "General Hospital" and in the feature film *Back to the Future*) to make her feel at ease in front of the camera without being in awe of it. Finding her older sister, who was expected to come of age in the series, proved to be a more difficult task for the producers. Hundreds of twelve- and thirteen-year-olds tried out for the part, but most of them "were already world-weary. We needed a young lady with spark," Thomason said. R.J. even admitted giving some thought to the possibility of casting one of his own daughters, but eventually decided he "would be crucified for nepotism."

When thirteen-year-old Samantha Smith showed up to audition, "we knew we'd found our Elizabeth," Thomason said. "She was inquisitive, polite, and quick to smile. And the most important thing was that she and R.J. hit it off from the start."

Samantha Smith, of course, was already well-known to Hollywood producers and the rest of America as the Maine schoolgirl who, in her concern about the possibility of nuclear war, had become pen-pals with Soviet Politburo Chairman Yuri Andropov. After touring the Kremlin at Andropov's invitation, and noting that the Russian people "were almost like Americans," Samantha had gained celebrity status on television talk shows and through her book, *Journey to the Soviet Union.* In 1984, she had hosted "Samantha Smith Goes to Washington: Campaign '84," a ninety-minute special in which she interviewed presidential candidates for cable TV's Disney Channel.

"After all she'd accomplished," Harry Thomason said, "Samantha was heady with the possibilities of what more she could do. She was not a jaded kid." In fact, after her audition, Samantha recalled, "I thought I did really terrible. I was in tears. Then Linda [co-producer Bloodworth-Thomason] came over and told me I had the series. I was thrilled."

Filming on "Lime Street," which also starred Lew Ayres as R.J.'s doting father, John Standing as R.J.'s dapper English partner, and Anne Haney as the Culver's housekeeper, proceeded smoothly for five episodes. "It's easy to work with someone who knows what he's doing," Samantha said about R.J. "He's like my own father. He helped me and Maia out a lot, giving us tips on acting. He's a sweet man, great with kids." The fact that the show was shot in various locations, including England, Bermuda, Washington, D. C., and the Virginia hunt country, also pleased Samantha, who felt lucky to have the chance to travel so widely.

In August 1985, Samantha and her father, Arthur, a former college professor, flew to London for scenes that had to be shot for upcoming episodes of "Lime Street." On August 25, on their return trip, Samantha, her father, and six other passengers were killed when the commuter plane they were on crashed thirty miles north of Portland, Maine.

The death of a child is always a tragic event, but Samantha's death touched the entire world, a world that had come to view her as a living symbol of what one concerned citizen, no matter how young, could do to make the world a better place to live. And in her death, she accomplished what she had not been able to in life: she brought the United States and Soviet Union together to talk of peace—if only for a brief moment.

At a memorial service held on August 28 at St. Mary's Church in Augusta, Maine, one thousand people came to mourn the schoolgirl who had softened the hearts in the Kremlin and won the love and respect of millions of people in both countries. Among the crowd was Soviet First Secretary for Cultural Affairs Vladimir Kulagin. "Samantha was a small ray of sunshine penetrating the thunderclouds of U. S.–Soviet relations," he said. "She instantly won us. She was so open and friendly. Maybe she did not understand what a good thing she was doing, when relations were so low. She was a small but great ambassador. And she showed us that this is not just a thing for diplomats."

R.J. flew in from Switzerland for the service. Visibly shaken, he escorted Samantha's mother, Jane Smith, into the crowded church. R.J. sat in the second pew, a row behind Mrs. Smith, and offered her comfort whenever she turned to him crying. He remained strong until they stood to sing "Let There Be Peace on Earth." R.J. stammered out the words and tears welled up in his eyes.

Later, he told reporters that he "adored that little girl. She had so much to live for. Everyone who came in contact with Samantha was left with something special." Remembering the last time he saw her, R.J. recalled that "she came to me with a copy of the script and asked me to sign it for her." It was one of the final episodes she filmed, in which a young classmate stands her up for the school dance. In the final poignant scene, R.J. waltzes her around the living room. "You didn't know your old dad had this many moves left, did you?"

"I knew," Samantha replied.

As they glided across the floor, they sang, "Because of you and me there will always be this moment in time."

At her memorial service, R.J. couldn't forget that particular scene. "I inscribed it for her. 'You know I love you,' I wrote. And I did. And I do. It's so hard to realize that suddenly someone so dear is gone."

His words speak a lifetime of similar realizations.

Postscript: "Lime Street" was cancelled in the winter of 1985. According to sources at Columbia Pictures, R.J. is considering other TV series. On March 3, 1986, he hosted a tribute to his first mentor, Spencer Tracy, at New York City's Majestic Theater. The circle, as they say, is unbroken.

Selected Filmography

The Happy Years (MGM, 1950)

Producer: Carey Wilson   _Director:_ William A. Wellman   _Screenplay:_ Harry Ruskin (from the _Lawrenceville School Stories_ by Owen Johnson)   _Photography:_ Paul C. Vogel   _Art Direction:_ Cedric Gibbons, Daniel B. Cathcart
Cast: Dean Stockwell, Darryl Hickman, Scotty Beckett, Leon Ames, Margalo Gillmore, Leo G. Carroll, Donn Gift, Peter Thompson, Jerry Mikelson, Alan Dinehart, Jr., David Blair, Danny Mummert, Addie LeRoy, George Chandler, Claudia Barrett, (with a walk-on by Robert Wagner)
Running Time: 110 minutes

Halls of Montezuma (20th Century-Fox, 1950)

Producer: Robert Bassler   _Director:_ Lewis Milestone   _Screenplay:_ Michael Blankfort   _Photography:_ Winton C. Hoch, Harry Jackson   _Music:_ Sol Kaplan   _Music Director:_ Lionel Newman
Cast: Richard Widmark, Jack Palance, Reginald Gardiner, Robert Wagner, Karl Malden, Richard Hylton, Richard Boone, Skip Homeier, Jack Webb, Bert Freed, Neville Brand, Don Hicks, Martin Milner
Running Time: 113 minutes

The Frogmen (20th Century-Fox, 1951)

Producer: Samuel G. Engel   _Director:_ Lloyd Bacon   _Screenplay:_ John Tucker Battle   _Photography:_ Norbert Brodine   _Music:_ Cyril Mockridge

Cast: Richard Widmark, Dana Andrews, Gary Merrill, Jeffrey Hunter, Warren Stevens, Robert Wagner, Harvey Lembeck
Running Time: 96 minutes

Let's Make It Legal (20th Century-Fox, 1951)

Producer: Robert Bassler *Director:* Richard Sale *Screenplay:* F. Hugh Herbert, I.A.L. Diamond *Photography:* Lucien Ballard *Musical Director:* Lionel Newman
Cast: Claudette Colbert, Macdonald Carey, Zachary Scott, Barbara Bates, Robert Wagner, Marilyn Monroe, Frank Cady, Jim Hayward, Carol Savage, Paul Gerrits, Betty Jane Bowen, Vici Raat, Ralph Sanford, Harry Denny, Harry Harvey, Sr.
Running Time: 77 minutes

With a Song in My Heart (20th Century-Fox, 1952)

Producer: Lamar Trotti *Director:* Walter Lang *Screenplay:* Lamar Trotti *Photography:* Leon Shamroy *Music Director:* Alfred Newman
Cast: Susan Hayward, David Wayne, Rory Calhoun, Thelma Ritter, Robert Wagner, Helen Westcott
Running Time: 117 minutes

What Price Glory? (20th Century-Fox, 1952)

Producer: Sol C. Siegel *Director:* John Ford *Screenplay:* Phoebe and Henry Ephron (based on the play by Maxwell Anderson and Lawrence Stallings) *Music:* Alfred Newman
Cast: James Cagney, Dan Dailey, Corinne Calvert, William Demarest, Robert Wagner, Marisa Pavan, James Gleason
Running Time: 111 minutes

Stars and Stripes Forever (20th Century-Fox, 1952)

Producer: Lamar Trotti *Director:* Henry Koster *Screenplay:* Lamar Trotti (from John Philip Sousa's autobiography) *Photography:*

Charles G. Clarke *Music Director:* Alfred Newman
Cast: Clifton Webb, Debra Paget, Robert Wagner, Ruth Hussey, Finlay
Currie, Roy Roberts, Lester Matthews
Running Time: 89 minutes

The Silver Whip (20th Century-Fox, 1953)

Producer: Robert Bassler, Michael Abel *Director:* Harmon Jones
Screenplay: Jesse Lassky, Jr. (based on the book by Jack Schaeffer)
Photography: Lloyd Ahern
Cast: Dale Robertson, Rory Calhoun, Robert Wagner, Kathleen Crow-
ley, James Millican, Lola Albright, J. M. Kerrigan, John Kellogg, Ian
MacDonald, Harry Carter, Robert Adler, Clancy Cooper, Burt Mus-
tin
Running Time: 73 minutes

Titanic (20th Century-Fox, 1953)

Producer: Charles Brackett *Director:* Jean Negulesco *Screenplay:*
Charles Brackett, Walter Reisch, Richard Breen *Photography:* Joe
MacDonald *Music:* Sol Kaplan *Art Direction:* Lyle Wheeler, Mau-
rice Ransford
Cast: Clifton Webb, Barbara Stanwyck, Robert Wagner, Audrey Dalton,
Thelma Ritter, Brian Aherne, Richard Basehart, Allyn Joslyn
Running Time: 98 minutes

Beneath the 12 Mile Reef (20th Century-Fox, 1953)

Producer: Richard Bassler *Director:* Robert D. Webb *Screenplay:*
A.I. Bezzerides *Photography:* Edward Cronjager *Music:* Bernard
Herrmann
Cast: Robert Wagner, Terry Moore, Gilbert Roland, Peter Graves, J.
Carrol Naish, Richard Boone, Angela Clarke, Jay Novello
Running Time: 102 minutes

Prince Valiant (20th Century-Fox, 1954)

Producer: Robert L. Jacks   *Director:* Henry Hathaway   *Screenplay:* Dudley Nicholls (based on the comic strip created by Harold Foster) *Photography:* Lucien Ballard   *Music:* Franz Waxman
Cast: Robert Wagner, James Mason, Debra Paget, Sterling Hayden, Victor McLaglen, Donald Crisp, Brian Aherne, Barry Jones, Primo Carnera
Running Time: 100 minutes

Broken Lance (20th Century-Fox, 1954)

Producer: Sol C. Siegel   *Director:* Edward Dmytryk   *Screenplay:* Richard Murphy (based on a short story by Philip Pordan)   *Photography:* Joe MacDonald
Cast: Spencer Tracy, Richard Widmark, Robert Wagner, Jean Peters, Katy Jurado, Earl Holliman, Hugh O'Brian, Eduard Franz, E.G. Marshall
Running Time: 96 minutes

White Feather (20th Century-Fox, 1955)

Producer: Robert L. Jacks   *Director:* Robert Webb   *Screenplay:* Delmer Daves, Leo Townshend   *Photography:* Lucien Ballard *Music:* Hugo Friedhofer
Cast: Robert Wagner, John Lund, Jeffrey Hunter, Debra Paget, Eduard Franz, Noah Beery, Jr., Hugh O'Brian, Virginia Leith, Emile Meyer
Running Time: 100 minutes

A Kiss Before Dying (United Artists, 1956)

Producer: Robert L. Jacks   *Director:* Gerd Oswald   *Screenplay:* Lawrence Roman (based on the novel by Ira Levin)   *Photography:* Lucien Ballard   *Music:* Lionel Newman
Cast: Jeffrey Hunter, Joanne Woodward, Robert Wagner, Virginia Leith, Mary Astor, George Macready
Running Time: 94 minutes

The Mountain (Paramount, 1956)

Producer: Edward Dmytryk   *Director:* Edward Dmytryk   *Screenplay:*
Ronald MacDougall (based on the novel by Henri Troyat)   *Photography:* Franz Planer   *Music:* Daniele Amfitheatrof
Cast: Spencer Tracy, Robert Wagner, Claire Trevor, William Demarest,
E.G. Marshall
Running Time: 105 minutes

The True Story of Jesse James (20th Century-Fox, 1956)

Producer: Herbert Swope, Jr.   *Director:* Nicholas Ray   *Screenplay:*
Walter Newman   *Photography:* Joe MacDonald   *Music:* Leigh Harline
Cast: Robert Wagner, Jeffrey Hunter, Hope Lange, Agnes Moorehead,
John Carradine, Alan Hale, Jr., Alan Baxter
Running Time: 92 minutes

The Hunters (20th Century-Fox, 1958)

Producer: Dick Powell   *Director:* Dick Powell   *Screenplay:* Wendell
Mayes   *Photography:* Charles G. Clarke   *Music:* Paul Sawtell
Cast: Robert Mitchum, Robert Wagner, Richard Egan, Mai Britt
Running Time: 108 minutes

In Love and War (20th Century-Fox, 1958)

Producer: Jerry Wald   *Director:* Philip Dunne   *Screenplay:* Edward
Anhalt (from the novel by Anton Myrer)   *Photography:* Leo Tover
Music: Hugo Friedhofer
Cast: Jeffrey Hunter, Robert Wagner, Bradford Dillman, Dana Wynter,
Hope Lange, Sheree North, France Nuyen
Running Time: 111 minutes

Say One for Me (20th Century-Fox, 1959)

Producer: Bing Crosby   *Director:* Frank Tashlin   *Screenplay:* Robert
O'Brien   *Photography:* Leo Tover   *Music Director:* Lionel Newman
(with songs by Sammy Cahn and James Van Heusen)
Cast: Bing Crosby, Robert Wagner, Debbie Reynolds, Ray Walston, Les
Tremayne, Connie Gilchrist, Frank McHugh, Joe Besser, Sebastian
Cabot
Running Time: 117 minutes

All the Fine Young Cannibals (MGM, 1960)

Producer: Pandro S. Berman   *Director:* Michael Anderson   *Screenplay:* Robert Thom (based on the novel *The Bixby Girls,* by Rosamond
Marshall)   *Photography:* William H. Daniels   *Music:* Jeff Alexander
Cast: Robert Wagner, Natalie Wood, Pearl Bailey, Susan Kohner,
George Hamilton, Jack Mullaney, Onslow Stevens, Anne Seymour
Running Time: 122 minutes

Sail a Crooked Ship (Columbia, 1961)

Producer: Philip Barry, Jr.   *Director:* Irving Brecher   *Screenplay:*
Ruth Brooks (from the novel by Nathaniel Benchley)   *Photography:*
Joseph Biroc   *Music:* George Duning
Cast: Robert Wagner, Ernie Kovacs, Dorothy Hart, Carolyn Jones,
Frank Gorshin
Running Time: 88 minutes

The Longest Day (20th Century-Fox, 1962)

Producer: Darryl F. Zanuck, Elmo Williams   *Director:* Andrew Martin, Ken Annakin, Bernhard Wicki   *Screenplay:* Cornelius Ryan, Romain Gary, James Jones, David Pursall, Jack Seddon (based on the
book by Cornelius Ryan)   *Photography:* Henri Persin, Walter Wottitz, Pierre Levent, Jean Bourgoin   *Music:* Maurice Jarre, Paul Anka
Cast: John Wayne, Robert Mitchum, Henry Fonda, Robert Ryan, Rod
Steiger, Robert Wagner, Paul Anka, Fabian, Tommy Sands, Richard
Beymer, Mel Ferrer, Jeffrey Hunter, Sal Mineo, Roddy MacDowall,

Stuart Whitman, Steve Forrest, Eddie Albert, Edmond O'Brien, Red Buttons, Tom Tryon, Alexander Knox, Ray Danton, Ron Randell, Richard Burton, Donald Houston, Kenneth More, Peter Lawford, Richard Todd, Leo Glenn, John Gregson, Sean Connery, Michael Medwin, Leslie Phillips, Irina Demich, Bourvil, Jean-Louis Barrault, Christian Marguand, Arletty, Curt Jurgens, Paul Hartmann, Gert Frobe, Wolfgang Preiss, Peter Van Eyck, Christopher Lee, Eugene Deckers, Richard Wattis
Running Time: 169 minutes

The War Lover (Columbia, 1962)

Producer: Arthur Hornblow, Jr. *Director:* Philip Leacock *Screenplay:* Howard Koch (based on the novel by John Hersey) *Photography:* Bob Huke *Music:* Richard Addinsell
Cast: Steve McQueen, Shirley Anne Field, Robert Wagner, Gary Cockrell, Michael Crawford
Running Time: 105 minutes

The Condemned of Altona (20th Century-Fox, 1962)

Producer: Carlo Ponti *Director:* Vittorio de Sica *Screenplay:* Abby Mann, Cesare Zavattinni (based on the play by Jean-Paul Sartre) *Photography:* Roberto Gerardi *Music:* Dmitri Shostakovich
Cast: Fredric March, Sophia Loren, Robert Wagner, Maximilian Schell, Françoise Prévost, Alfredo Franchi
Running Time: 113 minutes

The Pink Panther (United Artists, 1963)

Producer: Martin Jurow *Director:* Blake Edwards *Screenplay:* Maurice Richlin, Blake Edwards *Photography:* Philip Lathrop *Music:* Henry Mancini *Art Direction:* Fernando Carrere *Animation:* DePatie–Freeling
Cast: David Niven, Peter Sellers, Capucine, Claudia Cardinale, Robert Wagner, Brenda de Banzie, Colin Gordon
Running Time: 113 minutes

Harper (Warner Bros., 1966)

Producer: Gershwin–Kastner *Director:* Jack Smight *Screenplay:* William Goldman (based on the novel *The Moving Target,* by Ross Macdonald) *Photography:* Conrad Hall *Music:* Johnny Mandel
Cast: Paul Newman, Lauren Bacall, Shelley Winters, Arthur Hill, Julie Harris, Janet Leigh, Pamela Tiffin, Robert Wagner, Robert Webber, Strother Martin
Running Time: 121 minutes

Banning (Universal, 1967)

Producer: Dick Berg *Director:* Ron Winston *Screenplay:* James Lee *Photography:* Loyal Griggs *Music:* Quincy Jones
Cast: Robert Wagner, Anjanette Comer, Jill St. John, Guy Stockwell, James Farentino, Susan Clark, Howard St. John, Mike Kellin, Sean Garrison, Gene Hackman
Running Time: 102 minutes

The Biggest Bundle of Them All (MGM, 1967)

Producer: Shaftel–Stewart *Director:* Ken Annakin *Screenplay:* Josef Shaftel, Sy Salkowitz *Photography:* Piero Portalupi *Music:* Riz Ortolani
Cast: Raquel Welch, Robert Wagner, Vittorio de Sica, Edward G. Robinson, Godfrey Cambridge, Davy Kaye
Running Time: 110 minutes

Don't Just Stand There (Universal, 1967)

Producer: Stan Margulies *Director:* Ron Winston *Screenplay:* Charles Williams (from his novel, *The Wrong Venus*) *Photography:* Milton Krasner *Music:* Nick Perito
Cast: Mary Tyler Moore, Robert Wagner, Barbara Rhodes, Glynis Johns, Harvey Korman
Running Time: 99 minutes

Winning (Universal, 1969)

Producer: Paul Newman, John Foreman   *Director:* James Goldstone
Screenplay: Howard Rodman   *Photography:* Richard Moore
Music: Dave Grusin
Cast: Paul Newman, Joanne Woodward, Richard Thomas, Robert Wagner, David Sheiner, Clu Gulager
Running Time:

The Towering Inferno (20th Century-Fox/Warner Bros., 1974)

Producer: Irwin Allen   *Director:* John Guillermin, Irwin Allen
Screenplay: Stirling Silliphant (based on the novel *The Tower*, by Richard Martin Stern, and the novel *The Glass Inferno*, by Thomas M. Scortia and Frank M. Robinson)   *Photography:* Fred Koenekamp
Music: John Williams   *Special Effects:* Bill Abbott   *Production Designer:* William Creber
Cast: Paul Newman, Steve McQueen, William Holden, Faye Dunaway, Fred Astaire, Susan Blakely, Richard Chamberlain, Robert Vaughn, Jennifer Jones, O. J. Simpson, Robert Wagner
Running Time: 165 minutes

Midway (Universal, 1976)

Producer: Walter Mirisch   *Director:* Jack Smight   *Screenplay:* Donald S. Sanford   *Photography:* Harry Stradling, Jr.   *Music:* John Williams
Cast: Charlton Heston, Henry Fonda, Robert Mitchum, Glenn Ford, Edward Albert, James Coburn, Hal Holbrook, Toshiro Mifune, Robert Wagner, Robert Webber, Ed Nelson, James Shigeta, Monte Markham, Christopher George, Glenn Corbett
Running Time: 131 minutes

The Concorde—Airport '79 (Universal, 1979)

Producer: Jennings Lang   *Director:* David Lowell Rich   *Screenplay:* Eric Roth (based on a story by Jennings Lang; inspired by the novel *Airport*, by Arthur Hailey)   *Photography:* Philip Lathrop

Cast: Alain Delon, Susan Blakely, Robert Wagner, Sylvia Kristel, George Kennedy, Eddie Albert, Bibi Andersson, John Davidson, Andrea Marcovicci, Martha Raye, Cicely Tyson, Jimmie Walker, David Warner, Mercedes McCambridge, Charo
Running Time: 123 minutes

Trail of the Pink Panther (MGM/UA, 1982)

Producer: Blake Edwards, Tony Adams   *Director:* Blake Edwards
Screenplay: Blake Edwards, Geoffrey Edwards   *Photography:* Dick Bush   *Music:* Henry Mancini
Cast: Peter Sellers, David Niven, Herbert Lom, Richard Mulligan, Joanna Lumley, Robert Wagner, Capucine, Robert Loggia, Harvey Korman, Burt Kwouk, Graham Stark, Peter Arne
Running Time: 97 minutes

Curse of the Pink Panther (MGM/UA, 1983)

Producer: Blake Edwards, Tony Adams   *Director:* Blake Edwards
Screenplay: Blake Edwards, Geoffrey Edwards   *Photography:* Dick Bush   *Music:* Henry Mancini
Cast: Ted Wass, David Niven, Robert Wagner, Herbert Lom, Joanna Lumley, Capucine, Robert Loggia, Harvey Korman, Burt Kwouk, Leslie Ash, Andre Maranne
Running Time: 109 minutes

I Am the Cheese (Almi Film Release, 1983)

Producer: David Lange   *Director:* Robert Jiras   *Screenplay:* David Lange, Robert Jiras (based on the novel by Robert Cormier)   *Photography:* David Quaid
Cast: Robert MacNaughton, Hope Lange, Don Murray, Robert Wagner, Cynthia Nixon, Lee Richardson, John Fiedler, Sudie Bond
Running Time: 95 minutes

Television

TV Movies

The Streets of San Francisco (1971)
City Beneath the Sea (1971)
The Cable Car Mystery (1971)
Killer By Night (1971)
Madame Sin (1971)
The Affair (1973)
Death at Love House (1976)
Cat on a Hot Tin Roof (1976)
To Catch a King (1984)

TV Series

"It Takes a Thief" (1968–1970)
"Colditz" (1972–1973)
"Switch" (1975–1976)
"Hart to Hart" (1979–1984)
"Lime Street" (1985)

Index